Mother
Africa's Table

Mother Africa's Table

A Collection of West African
and African American Recipes and Cultural Traditions

The National Council of Negro Women, Inc.

Compiled by
Cassandra Hughes Webster

MAIN
STREET
BOOKS

An Ellen Rolfes Book

Main Street Books/Doubleday
New York   London   Toronto   Sydney   Auckland

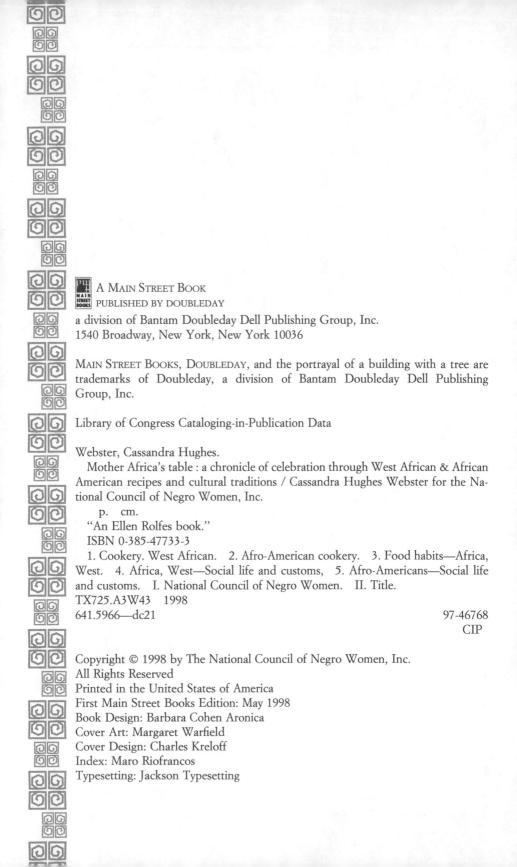

A MAIN STREET BOOK
PUBLISHED BY DOUBLEDAY
a division of Bantam Doubleday Dell Publishing Group, Inc.
1540 Broadway, New York, New York 10036

MAIN STREET BOOKS, DOUBLEDAY, and the portrayal of a building with a tree are trademarks of Doubleday, a division of Bantam Doubleday Dell Publishing Group, Inc.

Library of Congress Cataloging-in-Publication Data

Webster, Cassandra Hughes.
    Mother Africa's table : a chronicle of celebration through West African & African American recipes and cultural traditions / Cassandra Hughes Webster for the National Council of Negro Women, Inc.
        p.   cm.
    "An Ellen Rolfes book."
    ISBN 0-385-47733-3
    1. Cookery. West African.   2. Afro-American cookery.   3. Food habits—Africa, West.   4. Africa, West—Social life and customs, 5. Afro-Americans—Social life and customs.   I. National Council of Negro Women.   II. Title.
TX725.A3W43   1998
641.5966—dc21   97-46768
                                                                                         CIP

First Main Street Books Edition: May 1998
Book Design: Barbara Cohen Aronica
Cover Art: Margaret Warfield
Cover Design: Charles Kreloff
Index: Maro Riofrancos
Typesetting: Jackson Typesetting

This book is dedicated to the women who symbolize the mission of the National Council of Negro Women: to empower and celebrate women . . . those who have come before us, those here now, those yet to be.

Contents

casseroles. Ginger-Roasted Fish, Lemon Rice–Stuffed Catfish, Fried Catfish, Crisp Oven-Baked Catfish, Tuna Poché in a Tomato Case, Skillet Turkey Hash, Jerked Chicken Breast, Peri-Peri Game Hens (Cornish Game Hens with Peri-Peri Barbecue Marinade), Chicken 'n Dumplings, Spicy Fried Chicken, Curried Lamb with Potatoes, Lamb-Stuffed Green Pawpaw, Osu Tsinalo (Broiled Beef Strips with Sautéed Mushrooms), Beef Pot Roast, Liver and Onions, Oven-Baked Spareribs, Barbecued Spareribs, Barbecued Pork Roast, Pork Barbecue Burgers, Coconut Shrimp and Jollof Rice, Tiébou-djen (Senegalese Fried Rice with Fish), Chicken Thighs in Steak Sauce with Seasoned Rice, Traditional Chicken and Shrimp with Spiced Jollof Rice, Spicy Nigerian Chicken with Spiced Jollof Rice, Shrimp and Chicken Casserole, Chicken with Spicy Couscous, and Baked Sliced Tongue.

toes, Green Tomato Pie, Zucchini Pie, Scalloped Summer Squash, Creamed Squash, Chile Sambal (Dark Chile Shrimp Condiment), Hummus (Chick-Pea Spread), Red Pepper Dipping Sauce, Bajia (Red Chile-Coconut Sauce), Alloko Sauce (Spicy Fish Sauce), Mixed Spice Blends, and Brenda's Special Meat Seasoning Rub.

The Voice of Mother Africa

As her children readied themselves for the ships that would sail them to parts hitherto unheard of and unknown, Mother Africa wept silently. "What," she cried, "can I say to them to help them survive in their new world? What can I say . . . What can I say?"

As she listened to the prayers of her children, she knew precisely what she would say to them. Speaking through her priestesses, Mother Africa imparted pearls of wisdom wrapped with gems of truth. She recited the proverbs of their ancestors, sang the songs of their gods, and told the story of a people's past with lessons for the future. When Mother Africa spoke to her children, she spoke of family, faith, tradition, memory, respect, dignity, empathy, and knowledge.

Shhh! Listen quietly and carefully with your innermost heart while Mother Africa speaks.

Introduction

THE STORY AND THE JOURNEY
by Jessica B. Harris

There is an island off the coast of Senegal, the westernmost point of Africa, called Gorée. It is a happy island of day-trippers and weekenders, but today's joy masked the immense sorrow of the island, for if the stones could speak, they would set up a keening wail that could be heard throughout the world. Gorée was not always a happy place. For centuries its pink-hued walls were the final sight of Mother Africa for thousands of her children who were ripped from their homeland and sent across the water to become African Americans. Mother Africa cried for her children but she knew that she was not abandoning them. Rather, she was giving them over to her older sisters, the Atlantic, whose waters cradled them. Some she rocked on the fetid ships as they crossed over to their new land, giving them what little peace they had on the horrible journey; others she hugged to her foamy bosom as they chose to voyage to the land of the ancestors. She nourished them and transformed them, and reminded them of their true mother on the other side. All the time she whispered into their ear the very food that was to enable them to survive. It is a reminder to us that no matter how far we've journeyed or what roads we have taken, we are all Mother Africa's children when we sit down at Mother Africa's table.

CHAPTER ONE

Menus for African Ceremonies

THE NAMING CEREMONY

A male child has been born into this world and is now eight days old, so a time has been set for the Yoruba ritual naming ceremony. The ceremony's purpose is threefold: to establish the child's character traits, to make a link between the child and community, and to affirm and assure. The community affirms its responsibility in the upbringing of the child; the child is assured that he will be welcome and will be cared for by his family and the community. The Baba Lawo, or high priest, will officiate at the joyous event. The child's aunt has gathered the ritual items to place on his tongue: hot pepper sauce, honey, water, salt, gin, and a piece of coconut. They are crucial in helping to establish desirable character traits for this new life. The child's grandmothers are preparing the celebration dishes for this great day. The child's aunt will wear a golden buba and matching knife, along with her best amber jewelry. The Naming Ceremony is among the most joyous of all because it welcomes a new, sweet spirit into the world.

JOLLOF RICE
CHACHANGA (SPICY MEAT KABOBS)
AKARA (SHRIMP AND BLACK-EYED PEA FRITTERS)
SWEET PEPPER SALAD
GINGER-ROASTED FISH
CHICKEN GROUNDNUT STEW WITH VEGETABLES
JAMMA JAMMA (SPICED GREENS)
CHILE SAMBAL (DARK CHILE SHRIMP CONDIMENT)
GINGER-CITRUS SPARKLER

BONE HOUSE

What a marvelous day! No one could ask for a better Bone House day. The second child is but four weeks old today and his family is celebrating his birth with the whole village. The little one is so sweet and so handsome even at this young age. He is well loved by all. Soon, friends and family will gather at his home and sing the songs of celebration that will officially welcome their little one. Still, much work is to be done. Family and friends have come to help prepare the foods they will serve to the well wishers. The food will be plentiful, in celebration of the new life and out of respect and appreciation for all the blessings that have been bestowed upon them. They are looking forward to telling the story of how this little one came to be. The kidding around is the most fun of all.

CHICKEN THIGHS IN STEAK SAUCE WITH SEASONED RICE
KONTOMIRÉ STEW (SPINACH LEAF SAUCE)
LAMB-STUFFED GREEN PAWPAW (PAPAYA)
AKARA (SHRIMP AND BLACK-EYED PEA FRITTERS)
OKRO (FRIED OKRA)
BANANA ICE CREAM
LEMONGRASS HERBAL TEA

AN EVERYDAY CELEBRATION OF THE FAMILY

The compound is alive with activity this morning. Everyone has a job to do and is doing it, from the grandparents to the littlest cousin. The older women are gathered at the outdoor kitchen preparing the day's main meal. The younger women, sisters and cousins, are just coming back from the marketplace with fresh meat, mudfish, and fruit. Vegetables and herbs have been gathered from the family garden plot. It is not unusual for several hours to be spent in preparation of the meal. This day will provide an opportunity for aunts, mother, sisters, and nieces to gossip, commiserate, and just plain enjoy life. The men, old and young, have been cultivating crops, building and repairing structures, and creating works of art in the native woods. It is simply another day, but still it is a day for rejoicing that everyone is alive and well.

CHICKEN BREAST IN OKRA-PALAVA SAUCE
LEMON RICE–STUFFED CATFISH
JOLLOF RICE
COLLARD GREENS AND NECKBONES
BLACK-EYED PEAS IN GROUNDNUT SAUCE
PINEAPPLE MILK SHERBET
GINGER-CITRUS SPARKLER

WATCH NIGHT

Ma Kima has just died. In the front room sits her funeral bier where she will rest while friends in the compound come to pay their respects. The friends will help the family sit and watch over her through the night. If any one of them should fall asleep during the wake-keeping time, shame would come down upon the family. It is a privilege and a duty to honor the dead in this way. It is also the family's duty to provide food to their friends through the night.

African Americans perform this ritual a little differently. It is the American custom for the friends to provide food and drink for the grieving family. But the Cameroonians give the family a chance to show gratitude to their friends for their help during watch night.

CHICKEN GROUNDNUT STEW WITH VEGETABLES
FRIED CATFISH
COCONUT SHRIMP AND JOLLOF RICE
ZUCCHINI PIE
PLANTAIN FUFU
CHIN-CHIN (SWEET PASTRY)
GINGER-CITRUS SPARKLER

MEMORIAL SERVICE

It is Memorial Day. Fifteen years ago today, a beloved great-uncle, brother to the family's grandmother, died after living to an age ripe with experience and generosity. The family will wear all white, showing their respect and solidarity for this beloved man as a people and as a family. After the service they will share treasured memories of their great-uncle, and there will be a feast. In honor of their great-uncle, his favorite foods will be served so that all will eat in his memory.

GAME HENS IN SMOTHERED ONION SAUCE
BLACK-EYED PEAS IN GROUNDNUT SAUCE
SMOTHERED CABBAGE
FRIED RICE WITH OKRA
HUMMUS (CHICK-PEA SPREAD)
PEANUT PUNCH

CHAPTER TWO

African American Celebrations

K W A N Z A A

This cultural observance for black Americans and others of African descent was created in 1966 by Maulana (Ron) Karenga, who is currently chairman of black studies of California State University in Long Beach. Kwanzaa means "first fruits of the harvest" in Kiswahili, but there is no festival of that name in any African society. Karenga chose Kiswahili, the lingua franca of much of East Africa, to emphasize that black Americans come from many parts of Africa. Karenga synthesized elements from many African harvest festivals to create a unique celebration that is now observed in some way by more than five million Americans.

Kwanzaa is celebrated December 26 through January 1. Each of these seven days coincides with Dr. Karenga's seven principles for family and community: Umoja (unity), Kujichagulia (self-determination), Ujima (collective work and responsibility), Ujamaa (cooperative economics), Nia (purpose), Kuumba (creativity), and Imani (faith).

This is the first year Kwanzaa is to be celebrated in one African American home where in the past friends and relatives would come to a Christmas Eve celebration to eat, share fellowship, and decorate the tree. The family has decided to also start a new tradition, celebrating the Nguzo Saba, or seven principles, of Kwanzaa.

The mother and daughter of the family spent some time searching for the perfect kinara. The kinara is the holder for the seven candles. It is made of wood and represents the foundation upon which families stood clinging to their faith and its rituals while in danger of being torn asunder. Placed in the kinara are the mishumaa saba, or seven candles—one black in the center representing the color of our skins and our unity as a people, three red on the left representing the blood we have shed in our struggles to survive and prosper, and three green on the right representing our hopes for the future. On each of the seven nights beginning on December 26, the family and friends will gather to light the mishumaa and to discuss and celebrate the principle for that day.

The setting for the gathering will be the dining room, where African artifacts, books about African heritage, and paintings by African American

artists will have been placed. Chairs for the family's ancestors flank the sideboard, where the kinara stands on the mkeka, or straw mat. Also arranged on the mkeka are the mazao (fruits and vegetables), which represent the rewards of the family's collective efforts, and an ear of corn, or muhindi, for each child. Nearby is the kikombe cha umoja, or unity cup, filled with water to use in the libation in honor of the ancestors.

Zawadi, handcrafted or cultural gifts, sit on the table and will be exchanged at the end of the ceremony. Then there will be a feast of traditional dishes.

As they stand around the Kwanzaa setting, people greet one another by asking "Habari gani? What's the news?" And they end the discussion of the principle for that day with "Harambee! Let's pull together!"

AMBROSIA

CALLALOO SOUP

CORN BREAD

CURRIED LAMB WITH POTATOES

SPICY FRIED CHICKEN

HONEY-GLAZED CARROTS AND RAISINS

EGGPLANT CASSEROLE

BANANA FRITTERS

LEMONGRASS HERBAL TEA

NEW YEAR'S DAY

The first visitor to cross the threshold today can mean good luck for the rest of the year. Start those resolutions. This can be the year to learn more about your heritage, get physically fit, volunteer more, enjoy life more, spend more time with the family, work harder to be happy with yourself.

New Year's Day is a great day for beginnings, a day to make resolutions, a day to put in action the principles from Kwanzaa, a day to examine the past and access future directions. Not only a new day, but a new year dawns. We can learn from past mistakes and go boldly into the future armed with the strength of lessons learned.

The first day of the New Year is always filled with promise. Let us not break this promise.

BLACK-EYED PEAS AND HAM HOCKS

EGUSI (SPICY GREENS IN A PUMPKIN SEED SAUCE)

CHICKEN WITH SPICY COUSCOUS

SMOTHERED CABBAGE

BOILED PLANTAINS

BAKED RICE-RAISIN PUDDING

GINGER-CITRUS SPARKLER

THE BAPTISM

The first grandchild on both sides of the family is to be baptized today. He has been long anticipated and joyously welcomed, this new son and heir apparent to a family steeped in love!

For his baptism, the child will wear his grandfather's christening robe, made by the grandfather's grandmother because he, too, was the first grandchild. When the minister calls for those who will work together to raise this child in the way of the faithful, there will be not two, not four, but more like a dozen family members and friends who will commit to this responsibility.

Their faith and commitment truly embody the African belief that it takes "a village to raise a child."

Of course, there will be a celebration after church. The grands and aunts have been cooking for two days in preparation for this occasion!

Welcome to the family, little one. You are truly loved.

JERKED CHICKEN BREAST
EXTRA-RICH HOMINY GRITS
JOLLOF RICE
FRIED GREEN TOMATOES
CORN PUDDING
KONTOMIRÉ WITH OKRA (STEAMED SPINACH WITH OKRA)
TROPICAL FRUIT DESSERT
ORANGE SPICE TEA

RITES OF PASSAGE

The brothers of Ndugu and the sisters of Nzinga will cross this evening. After a year-long journey filled with study, exploration, and examination, the ritual of this evening will mark the crossings of boys to men and girls to women so that they may be productive in their roles as leaders and nurturers.

Forever laid aside are little-boy ways, thoughts, and deeds. Fully embraced is the knowledge that they are men responsible for their actions and the effects of those actions. They are crossing together as brothers, so they will know that they are not alone and have others to count on when times are difficult.

This evening they will wear clothing that reflects their African heritage. They will paint their bodies and carry staffs. Singing, dancing, and chanting, they will give voice to their new status. Gifts, handcrafted and chosen with love, will be presented to them, and they will make presentations to Baba (father leader), to their elders, and to each other.

The ritual of the crossing will take several hours, but it culminates, as most celebrations do, with a feast. Those who are crossing and those who have come to participate in the celebration have a chance to sample a little of everything that has been prepared for the meal. Those crossing are, in fact, the last to eat, so they may feel hunger pangs even after partaking. That's because the purpose of the feast is but an extension of the ritual, breaking bread and sharing in bounty. The ritual of the crossing represents realized potential.

CHACHANGA (SPICY MEAT KABOBS)
CHICKEN GROUNDNUT SOUP—THE GHANAIAN WAY
OKRA BEEF SAUCE
BOILED WHITE RICE
ALLOKO (FRIED PLANTAINS)
FESTIVE CORN AND BLACK-EYED PEA SALAD
SWEET POTATO PONE
WEST AFRICAN FRUIT PUNCH

G R A D U A T I O N

Another college graduate! It's been a struggle financially at times, academically at times, but it's almost over. The mortarboard will be tossed in the air, smiles will be broad, pride will be apparent.

After the ceremony, friends and family will go to the rented hall where major celebrating will take place. The deejay is warming up. The place is balloon-filled. The father of the honoree insisted on a caterer that served "soul food." As a matter of fact, he has had more fun than anyone else, going on taste tests to select the perfect caterer, and for sure, he is going to make certain that there is plenty of good food.

Gifts for the new graduate might include cash, jewelry, a trip to the Bahamas, a new car, a computer—the sky's the limit in the gifts the graduate will receive, and the sky's the limit in the opportunities the graduate will pursue.

Graduation day is a momentous day in any family, but particularly in the African American family. It represents the fruit of many labors to ensure the right to an education, the right to equal opportunity, and the right to choose a career.

On some diplomas you can still see faint traces of the blood shed by former slaves and African ancestors who survived the Middle Passage. They represent a strong legacy and an even stronger future.

PERI-PERI GAME HENS
SHRIMP AND CHICKEN CASSEROLE
BAKED SAUSAGE AND RICE
GREEN TOMATO PIE
AFRICAN CABBAGE SALAD
OLD-FASHIONED CARAMEL CAKE
BAKED BANANA DESSERT
ORANGE SPICE TEA

THE WEDDING

Something old, something new, something borrowed, something blue. Traditional or African? Or parts of both? What type of music? From where to select the readings? Do we go with Kente cloth for the groomsmen's cummerbunds and bow ties, or not? Southern belle or African princess? Who will cater? Deejay or live band? These are the questions the daughter of the family pondered as she planned her wedding day.

At last the day was here, and her choices were perfect for what she wanted to evoke—a nineties African American woman looking to her future but strongly rooted in her past, her heritage.

She finally decided to go with a traditionally styled dress made of ivory-colored African cloth with gold thread and matching gele, or headdress. Instead of roses and carnations, the church was decorated with palms and tropical flowers. Kente cloth draped the pews where the parents sat, and the groom and his groomsmen went with the Kente cloth cummerbunds and bow ties.

The wedding service culminated with the bride and groom "jumping the broom" in remembrance of the slave families who clung to their faith and its rituals while in danger of being torn asunder.

The reception buffet was a smorgasbord of African and African American foods, lovingly and expertly prepared by an aunt and uncle of the bride who own a restaurant and catering business.

AVOCATS AUX CREVETTES (AVOCADO-SHRIMP APPETIZER)
AFRICAN SEAFOOD SOUP
BEEF POT ROAST
TIÉBOU-DJEN (SENEGALESE FRIED RICE WITH FISH)
SUGAR SNAP PEA SALAD
TUWO GINKAFA (MASHED RICE)
LAMB AND EGGPLANT SAUCE
ALLOKO (FRIED PLANTAINS)
WEDDING CAKE
GINGER BEER

FAMILY REUNION

The Jeffries-Carrington family T-shirts were delivered yesterday, and they look great! They are black with the family names in red and gold silkscreen and an extended family depicted in gold. The reunion is scheduled for the 21st of the month.

Cousin Hortense is flying from Barbados with her husband and daughters. Grandma Lottie, who will be ninety-six years old in September, will be there to meet and greet old and new family members. Uncle Jake will be there with his blues guitar, and for the first time, the reunion will embrace six generations, from Grandma Lottie down to eight-week-old Mustapha, all gathered to celebrate the family's survival and success.

The park pavilion and picnic area have been reserved, and everyone prays that the weather will be fine. There are enough grills in the picnic area for the "chefs," and Aunt Jan is in charge of the family games.

Various relatives will be bringing favorite dishes. A family reunion is a time for the whole clan to gather together and recommit and rededicate themselves to each other as well as plan for the future generations. Being with the family renews the soul and refreshes the spirit. It also adds about six pounds to the figure—unless it gets worked off in the sack races.

BARBECUED SPARERIBS
FRIED CATFISH
RED BEANS AND RICE
CORN BREAD
SCALLOPED SUMMER SQUASH
SWEET PEPPER SALAD
MARINATED AFRICAN FRUIT SALAD
VINEGAR PIE
WATERMELON-GINGER REFRESHER

THE WAKE

It is always difficult to say farewell to someone who has played such a large role in so many lives. T'ant June lived through a lot of history: Klan lynchings, two World Wars, the Depression, Freedom Rides, the Riots of '69, the Million-Man March.

She raised four children of her own and another twenty nieces, nephews, and neighborhood children. There was a neighborhood young man who was dying of AIDS, and T'ant June would go to his home every afternoon to give his mother a break from caring for him. She would bathe and feed him and read to him.

Along the tables of food at her sister T'ant Irene's house, each of the family members and friends in turn remembers the spirit that was T'ant June: her sayings, her temper, her songs, and her cooking. She made wine in her basement—fine wine too!

No one asks for any of her possessions because everyone has a piece of her resting already in his soul. Her physical self will be missed, but not her spirit. It's here and all around.

CHICKEN THIGHS IN STEAK SAUCE WITH SEASONED RICE
BANKU (CORNMEAL DUMPLINGS)
OSU TSINALO (BROILED BEEF STRIPS WITH SAUTÉED
MUSHROOMS)
BAKED SLICED TONGUE
BOILED WHITE RICE
YAM AND SWEET POTATO FUFU
JAMMA JAMMA (SPICED GREENS)
THIAKRY (CHAKREY)
GINGER BEER

KNOWLEDGE

One good way to really get to know and connect with someone is to invite him or her to dinner. Sitting across the table from one another, sharing experiences, thoughts, and feelings as well as food is a way of creating community and making connections. Just as food provides the energy needed to create and connect, so too does knowledge play a role in creativity and connection. Knowledge is empowering. Withhold knowledge and you withhold power from a people. Withhold food and you kill a people. If we think of knowledge as we do food, we see that food gives us energy and energy gives us strength. What is knowledge if not strength? Knowledge is like the communal cup of palm wine. Hoarded, it turns into vinegar; shared, it is the nectar of the gods. The pursuit of knowledge defines our humanness, but it is the sharing of knowledge that defines our humanity.

CHAPTER THREE

Beverages and Openers

Although climate dictates the
tradition of beverages, African culinary
creativity has produced an abundance
of tropical fruit-, herb-,
and nut-flavored drinks.

Watermelon-Ginger Refresher

1 medium ripe watermelon, rind removed, seeded and cut into large chunks (about 8 cups)
2 cups water
⅓ to ½ cup granulated sugar, depending on desired sweetness
⅓ cup grated fresh gingerroot
Crushed ice

In small batches, blend 6½ cups of the watermelon chunks with the water, sugar, and ginger until smooth. Pour the watermelon purée into a serving pitcher. Chop the remaining 1½ cups of watermelon chunks and add to the pitcher. Refrigerate until well chilled. (Do not add ice to chill, as this will dilute the flavor.) When ready to serve, stir and pour the refresher over crushed ice.

HINT: To grate the ginger, cut away any shriveled or dried portions of the bulb. Scrape the unpeeled ginger against a spiked ceramic or metal ginger grater (which breaks rather than tears the fibers) or against the finest grids of a metal grater. Be sure to capture all the juices and pulp. Ground dried ginger does not have the same fresh, intense flavor as fresh ginger and is not an appropriate substitute.

FRESH GINGER has a peppery, slightly sweet flavor with an exotic spicy fragrance. Look for fresh gingerroot (it actually is an underground stem) in the specialty produce section of your supermarket. Select ginger that is rock hard with a smooth light-tan skin pulled tautly over the bulb. Cut away all sections that are shriveled, soft, or dried out before grating.

MAKES ABOUT 2 QUARTS

Ginger Beer

¾ cup (4 ounces) grated fresh gingerroot (see notes page 20)
2 tablespoons fresh-squeezed lime juice
½ teaspoon cream of tartar
12 cups (3 quarts) plus ¼ cup water
2 (¼-ounce) packages active dry yeast
2 cups granulated sugar, divided

1. In a large nonreactive bowl, whisk together the grated gingerroot, lime juice, and cream of tartar. In a large pot, bring 12 cups of the water to a boil over high heat. Remove from the heat and carefully pour the hot water over the ginger mixture. Set aside to cool.

2. In a separate bowl, stir together the yeast, remaining ¼ cup of water, and ½ cup of the sugar to make a smooth paste. When the ginger mixture is lukewarm, add the yeast mixture and stir well to blend. Cover the bowl loosely with plastic wrap and let stand for 3 days in a cool room.

3. Pour the ginger mixture through a sieve into a large pitcher. Discard the grated gingerroot. Add the remaining 1½ cups sugar, stirring until dissolved. Refrigerate until chilled. Serve the ginger beer over ice.

MAKES ABOUT 3 QUARTS OR 12 CUPS

Orange Spice Tea for a Crowd

1 gallon (16 cups) water
6 oolong or orange-pekoe tea bags
1½ cups orange juice, prepared from frozen concentrate or fresh squeezed
2½ cups granulated sugar
Mint sprigs

1. Heat the water to boiling in a large pot. Add the tea bags, lower the heat and simmer uncovered for 10 minutes. Remove the pot from the heat and let stand for 10 minutes. Remove and discard the tea bags.

2. Add the orange juice and sugar to the hot tea, stirring until the sugar has dissolved. Serve hot, garnished with mint, or chill and serve over ice.

VARIATION: Add an assortment of aromatic spices to the boiling water (allspice, cinnamon sticks, nutmeg, cloves) and use herbal tea bags in place of the black tea for an entirely different-flavored tea.

MAKES ABOUT 16 CUPS

West African Fruit Punch

2½ cups lemonade prepared from frozen concentrate
1 cup pineapple juice
1 cup guava nectar or juice
1 cup orange juice
1 cup papaya nectar or juice
Pineapple wedges and maraschino cherries or fresh strawberries to garnish

In a large pitcher, mix the lemonade with the pineapple juice, guava nectar, orange juice, and papaya nectar. Refrigerate until chilled. Serve over ice, garnished with a pineapple wedge skewered with a cherry or strawberry.

VARIATION: Add ⅓ cup of the syrup from bottled maraschino cherries for a slightly different flavor and color.

MAKES 6½ CUPS

Lemongrass Herbal Tea

1 pound fresh lemongrass, rinsed and cut into 4-inch pieces
6 cups water
Granulated sugar to taste (about ⅓ cup plus 2 tablespoons)
Handful of fresh herbs (mint, basil, or sorrel leaves) plus additional for garnish

1. Remove a layer of the tough outer lemongrass stalks (leaves) and trim away the tops of the stalks to yield about twelve 8-inch-long pieces with small bulblike bases. Slice each stalk diagonally into 4-inch-long portions. You should have about 2 cups.

2. In a teapot or saucepan, bring the water to a boil. Drop in the lemongrass. Remove from the heat, cover, and steep for 10 minutes.

3. Add sugar to taste, stirring to completely dissolve. Crush the herbs and stir into the lemongrass tea. Refrigerate until chilled. When ready to serve, place a few of the remaining fresh herb leaves and some ice cubes in tall beverage glasses. Pour the tea through a strainer into the glasses and serve.

LEMONGRASS: is a fragrant herb sold by the stalk in small bundles. The stalks have a fibrous, almost woody texture with a subtle citrus scent.

MAKES ABOUT 6 CUPS

Peanut Punch

½ to ⅔ cup smooth peanut butter
3 cups cold whole milk
4 to 6 tablespoons granulated sugar
⅛ teaspoon ground cinnamon
⅛ teaspoon freshly grated nutmeg
4 to 6 ice cubes

Place ½ cup of the peanut butter, the milk, sugar, cinnamon, nutmeg, and ice cubes in a blender container and process on high speed for about 30 seconds, until thick and frothy. Sample the punch, adding up to ⅓ cup additional peanut butter and/or sugar to taste. Pour into tall chilled glasses and serve immediately.

VARIATION: Reduce milk to 1½ cups and add 2 scoops of vanilla or chocolate ice cream. Follow the recipe as directed.

NOTE: To grate nutmeg, place the brown kernel against the surface of a nutmeg grater or against the finest grids of a metal grater. Rub the nutmeg over the surface, being careful not to scrape your knuckles.

NUTMEG is sold either as a hard brown egg-shaped kernel about 1 inch in length or commercially ground. Whole nutmeg freshly ground with a grater is superior in flavor and aroma to packaged ground nutmeg.

MAKES 4 CUPS

Ginger-Citrus Sparkler

I cup grated fresh gingerroot
½ cup fresh-squeezed lemon or grapefruit juice (about 3 lemons)
1½ cups pineapple juice, prepared from frozen concentrate
I cup orange juice, prepared from frozen concentrate
4 cups water
Sugar to taste (about ⅓ cup)
Lemon-lime-flavored soft drink or sparkling water
Orange or lemon spices (optional)

1. In a pitcher, combine the ginger with the lemon, pineapple, and orange juices. Stir in the water and refrigerate until chilled.

2. Before serving, add the sugar to taste, stirring to dissolve completely. To serve, fill a tall beverage glass with ice cubes. Pour the sparkler halfway up the glass. Fill and top off with soda or sparkling water. Garnish with a fresh orange or lemon slice, if desired.

VARIATION: Omit the soda, reduce the ginger to 2 tablespoons, and serve as a citrus juice blend over crushed ice.

MAKES 2 QUARTS

Chachanga
(Spicy Meat Kabobs)

GHANA/
TOGO

1 teaspoon ground red pepper (cayenne) or paprika
1 tablespoon Mixed Spice (see page 164)
½ teaspoon salt
¼ cup roasted groundnuts (peanuts), ground into powder
2 tablespoons vinegar
1 pound mutton, liver, or beef, sliced into ⅜ x 8-inch strips or cubed
1 onion, cut into pieces for skewering
2 tablespoons vegetable oil
½ cup crushed roasted groundnuts (optional)

1. In a small bowl, mix together the cayenne, mixed spice, salt, powdered groundnuts, and vinegar to make a paste. Place the meat and
paste in a sealable plastic bag and massage the paste into the meat until
evenly covered. Seal the bag and refrigerate for at least 6 hours or
overnight.

2. Prepare a hot charcoal fire. Soak twelve 6-inch bamboo skewers in
water for 30 minutes. Thread the meat and onion on skewers. Sprinkle
the meat with oil and grill over hot coals for approximately 3 to 5 minutes on each side, depending on the thickness of the meat and the
desired degree of doneness. Roll the cooked skewers in crushed
groundnuts before serving, if desired.

SERVING SUGGESTION: Serve with Jollof Rice and Red Pepper Dipping Sauce (see pages 123 and 161), or enjoy as an appetizer with relish
or hot pepper sauce or as an entree with a salad, rice, and bread.

(continued on next page)

HINT: To prepare groundnut powder, place roasted peanuts in a cleaned coffee grinder and pulverize.

MAKES 8 KABOBS

Sausage Meatballs

1 pound bulk pork sausage
1 egg, slightly beaten
1/3 cup bread crumbs
1/2 teaspoon ground red pepper (cayenne)
1 cup ketchup
1/3 cup packed brown sugar
2 tablespoons cider vinegar
2 tablespoons soy sauce

1. Mix together the sausage, egg, bread crumbs, and cayenne until well blended. Form into 24 small balls. Set aside.

2. Combine the ketchup, brown sugar, vinegar, and soy sauce in a non-reactive skillet and stir to thoroughly blend. Bring to a boil. Add the meatballs, reduce the heat, cover, and cook over medium heat for 30 minutes, stirring occasionally. If the sauce begins to thicken or burn, stir in 1 to 2 tablespoons of water.

MAKES 2 DOZEN COCKTAIL MEATBALLS

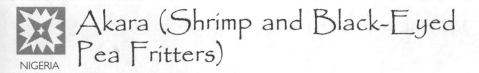

Akara (Shrimp and Black-Eyed Pea Fritters)

¾ pound dried black-eyed peas (about 1½ cups)
Water
1 cup finely chopped yellow onion
2 red jalapeño chile peppers, seeded and minced
1 tablespoon salt
2 eggs, beaten
1 cup shredded smoked salmon or herring or 2 tablespoons dried shrimp
   powder
Peanut (groundnut) oil for deep-frying
Red Pepper Dipping Sauce (see page 161)

1. Rinse the black-eyed peas and sort through them to remove any grit or small stones. Place the peas in a pot and cover with 3 times the amount of cold water. Loosely cover the pot with plastic wrap and allow the peas to soak overnight. If the peas are not soft when squeezed between fingers, place in simmering water for 15 minutes. Immediately remove from the heat and drain. (Do not boil or overcook or the peas will absorb too much water. If this occurs, begin the recipe over.)

2. If desired, rub the peas between your hands under running water to remove the skins and the black spots, or eyes. In small batches, place the peas in a blender container with up to ¼ cup of water and purée into a smooth paste. Using a spatula, remove the paste from the blender into a mixing bowl. Repeat the process until all the peas are puréed. Blend the onion and chile peppers until smooth (using a little water if necessary). Mix the blended onion mixture and salt into the puréed peas. Adjust seasoning to taste.

3. Using an electric mixer, slowly mix the batter on the lowest setting, moving in a clockwise or counterclockwise motion to incorporate as much air into the mixture as possible. Add the eggs and continue mix-

ing for 3 minutes, until thoroughly blended. Stir in the salmon and refrigerate for 10 minutes.

4. Fill a large heavy pot or a deep-fat fryer with oil to come no more than halfway up the side. Heat the oil to 375° or 380°F. Using a small ice cream scoop or spoon, carefully drop the batter into the hot oil. Fry the fritters in small batches for about 4 minutes or until golden brown, turning once. Remove with a slotted spoon and drain on absorbent towels.

SERVING SUGGESTION: Serve as a breakfast dish with hot Pap (see page 139) or serve as an appetizer with Red Pepper Dipping Sauce.

MAKES 20 FRITTERS

MEMORY

The smell of freshly baked bread can evoke powerful memories. That aroma can send someone back in time to a long-ago Sunday morning when a grandmother was putting the final touches on the family dinner. There lives in all of us an individual memory, whether of a treasured relative, a favorite song, a delicious meal. There also lives in all of us a family memory, or being a part of something larger than ourselves. And there lives in all of us a collective memory, of greatness, joyousness, spiritedness. Our memories are our interpretations of our history as a people. Roll them around the palate of your mind and savor their richness. Memories are comfort food for the soul.

CHAPTER FOUR

Salads, Soups, and Breads

Home-style West African culinary
tradition does not emphasize first
courses of either appetizers or salads.
Yet when entertaining, the hostess
sets out a lavish spread of a variety of
salads and hors d'oeuvres.

Avocats aux Crevettes
(Avocado-Shrimp Appetizer)

1½ cups water
12 medium uncooked shrimp, shelled and deveined, tails left on
Salt
2 large ripe avocados
2 tablespoons lemon juice
2 tablespoon tomato paste
5 tablespoons mayonnaise
½ teaspoon ground red pepper (cayenne) or ½ teaspoon hot sauce or minced
   canned chile chipotle
Salad greens (optional)
Minced parsley and lemon wedges to garnish

1. In a small saucepan, bring the water to a boil. Add the shrimp and
½ teaspoon of salt. Return to a boil, cover the saucepan, and remove
from the heat. Let stand 3 minutes or until the shrimp are completely
pink and just cooked. Drain. Cover the shrimp to keep warm.

2. Place the avocados on a cutting board and slice them lengthwise.
Separate the halves and remove the pits. Sprinkle the cavities with salt
and 1 tablespoon of lemon juice; set aside.

3. In a small bowl, whisk together the tomato paste, the remaining tablespoon of lemon juice, the mayonnaise, and the cayenne until blended.
Cover and refrigerate until ready to assemble.

4. To serve, arrange the avocado halves on a bed of salad greens, if desired. Place 3 shrimp in each avocado cavity. Top with the spicy mayonnaise and lightly sprinkle with minced parsley. Garnish with lemon wedges and serve.

SENEGAL

SERVES 4

Garden Greens with Hot Bacon Dressing

3 slices bacon, cut into 1-inch pieces
1 tablespoon flour
2 tablespoons sugar
1½ teaspoons coarsely ground black pepper
1 egg, beaten
¼ cup cider vinegar
1 cup water
Salt
1 bunch dandelion greens, rinsed and chilled
1 bunch baby spinach leaves, rinsed and chilled
½ small red onion, sliced thin
2 hard-cooked eggs, chopped

1. Fry the bacon in a heavy skillet over medium-high heat until completely crisp. Remove the bacon from the drippings and drain on absorbent towels. Crumble when cool and set aside.

2. In a small bowl, mix together the flour, sugar, and pepper. Whisk in the egg, vinegar, and water until well blended. Reheat the bacon drippings over a medium flame until warmed. Slowly pour the flour mixture into the hot drippings, while constantly stirring. Cook until slightly thickened. Season to taste with salt, if desired.

3. Arrange the greens on a serving platter. Pour the hot dressing over the greens, tossing to coat. Garnish with the onion, hard-cooked eggs, and reserved crumbled bacon. Serve immediately.

SERVES 4

Sugar Snap Pea Salad

AFRICAN
AMERICAN

2 (10-ounce) packages frozen sugar snap peas
1 (15-ounce) can red kidney beans, drained and rinsed
½ cup pitted and sliced black olives
4 to 5 green onion stalks, sliced fine
1 red bell pepper, cored and diced
1 to 2 jalapeño chile peppers, seeded and slivered
1 cup granulated sugar
½ cup red wine vinegar
½ cup apple cider vinegar
¼ cup minced parsley
¼ cup extra-virgin olive oil
½ teaspoon salt
½ teaspoon dried basil leaves
½ teaspoon dried oregano leaves
1 to 2 teaspoons hot pepper sauce
Lettuce leaves (butterleaf or curly endive), separated, rinsed, and chilled

1. Cook the sugar snap peas as directed on the package; drain. Do not overcook. Immediately rinse under cold running water and place in a colander. Shake to drain excess water.

2. Combine the sugar snap peas, kidney beans, olives, green onion, bell pepper, and chile pepper in a large mixing bowl.

3. In a small bowl, whisk together the sugar, wine vinegar, cider vinegar, parsley, olive oil, salt, basil, and oregano until most of the sugar is dissolved. Add up to 2 teaspoons hot sauce to taste. Pour the dressing over the salad and toss to coat the vegetables. Refrigerate for 8 hours, tossing the salad a few times. Serve chilled on lettuce leaves.

SERVES 6 TO 8

African Cabbage Salad

¼ head red cabbage, coarsely chopped (about 2 cups)
¼ head green cabbage, coarsely chopped (about 2 cups)
½ bunch parsley, chopped (about I cup)
I cucumber, scored with a fork, halved lengthwise, and sliced (about 2 cups)
I small red onion, sliced into short strips (about I cup)

VINAIGRETTE DRESSING
¾ cup vegetable or light olive oil
⅓ cup red wine vinegar
I teaspoon Maggi's seasoning or Worcestershire sauce
2 large cloves garlic, flattened
½ teaspoon dry mustard
½ teaspoon salt
¼ teaspoon ground black pepper or red chili powder

1. In a salad bowl, toss together the cabbage, parsley, cucumber, and red onion; cover and refrigerate. Makes 8 cups.

2. Make the vinaigrette: Combine the oil, vinegar, Maggi's, garlic, mustard, salt, and black pepper in a jar with a tight-fitting lid. Cover tightly and shake until blended. Refrigerate at least 1 hour. Makes 1 cup.

3. Fifteen minutes before serving, shake the bottled dressing. Remove and discard the garlic. Pour the dressing over the cabbage salad, tossing to mix well. Cover and let sit 5 minutes to absorb the flavors. Toss once again before serving.

SERVES 6 to 8

Sweet Pepper Salad

2 (6-ounce) bags spinach leaves
1 red bell pepper, cored, seeded, and sliced into short strips (about 1 cup)
1 green bell pepper, cored, seeded, and sliced into short strips (about 1 cup)
1 small yellow onion, sliced thin (about 1 cup)
⅓ cup olive oil
3 tablespoons red wine vinegar
¼ to ½ teaspoon red chili powder
½ teaspoon Mixed Spice (see page 164) or garlic powder
¼ teaspoon salt
2 ripe avocados, peeled and sliced lengthwise
3 hard-cooked eggs, quartered
1 cup Kuli-Kuli (see page 54), broken into pieces, or 1 cup crushed roasted
   peanuts

1. Prepare the salad ingredients: Rinse, drain, spin dry, and destem the
spinach leaves. Coarsely tear them into bite-size pieces and place in a
mixing bowl with the peppers and onion. Cover and refrigerate.

2. In a small bowl, whisk together the oil, vinegar, chili powder, mixed
spice, and salt. Let the dressing stand for at least 1 hour.

3. Before serving, pour the dressing over the salad ingredients and toss.
Arrange the avocado and egg slices over the salad and top with kuli-
kuli (peanut "croutons"). Serve immediately.

SERVES 6

Black-Eyed Pea Salad

2 (8-ounce) cans black-eyed peas, drained

1 (16-ounce) can Ro-Tel diced tomatoes and green chile or 1 cup diced tomato
and ¼ cup canned diced green chile

3 stalks green onions (scallions), sliced

½ cup sliced black olives

1 cup bottled Italian dressing

4 ounces feta cheese, crumbled (about 1 cup)

Frito-brand corn chips

Combine the black-eyed peas, tomatoes and green chile, green onions, and black olives in a mixing bowl. Pour in the dressing and toss to mix well. Refrigerate at least 5 hours or overnight. Before serving, stir in the feta cheese and corn chips. Serve immediately.

SERVES 4

Festive Corn and Black-Eyed Pea Salad

1 (14½-ounce) can corn kernels, drained
1 (15-ounce) can black-eyed peas, rinsed and drained
½ cup thinly sliced celery
1 medium red bell pepper, cored, seeded, and chopped
4 green onions (scallions), sliced thin
¼ cup vegetable or salad oil
3 tablespoons red wine vinegar
2 teaspoons honey
1 teaspoon fresh lemon juice
½ teaspoon salt
½ teaspoon ground black pepper
½ teaspoon red chili powder

1. In a large bowl, combine the corn, peas, celery, bell pepper, and green onions. Set aside.

2. Combine the oil, vinegar, honey, lemon juice, salt, pepper, and chili powder in a tightly covered container and shake until the dressing is well blended. Pour the dressing over the vegetables and toss well. Cover and refrigerate at least 1 hour, stirring occasionally. Toss before serving.

SERVES 4

24-Hour Potato and Cabbage Salad

10 medium russet potatoes, scrubbed
1 (32-ounce) container mayonnaise (4 cups)
1 tablespoon celery seeds
½ teaspoon salt
1 teaspoon ground black pepper
½ head green cabbage, shredded (about 4 cups)
½ head red cabbage, shredded (about 4 cups)
6 green onions (scallions), sliced (about 1 cup)
2 green bell peppers, cored, seeded, and chopped
Paprika
3 hard-cooked eggs, sliced

1. Place the potatoes in salted water to cover. Bring to a vigorous boil, lower the heat to medium, and cook 30 minutes, or until tender when pierced with a fork. Drain and let cool. Peel and cut into small chunks.

2. Place the potatoes in a large mixing bowl with 3 cups of the mayonnaise, the celery seeds, salt, and black pepper; gently toss to cover evenly. Stir in the cabbage, onions, and bell pepper. Mix thoroughly.

3. Spread the remaining 1 cup of mayonnaise over the top of the salad and sprinkle generously with paprika. Tightly cover and refrigerate for 24 hours. Decorate with the egg slices before serving.

SERVES 20 to 25

Picnic Potato Salad

AFRICAN
AMERICAN

6 white or red boiling potatoes
½ cup mayonnaise
¼ cup prepared mustard
¼ cup chopped white onion
¼ cup chopped celery
¼ cup chopped pimento-stuffed green olives
¼ cup sweet pickle relish
¼ cup sweet pickle juice
2 hard-cooked eggs, chopped
Salt and ground black pepper
Paprika to garnish

1. Scrub the potatoes. Place in a pot with cold salted water to cover. Bring to a boil, then reduce the heat slightly and gently boil, partially covered, until tender when pierced with a knife, about 15 to 30 minutes depending on size. Drain and set aside to cool. Pull off the skins and dice into bite-size chunks.

2. In a mixing bowl, combine the mayonnaise, mustard, onion, celery, pickle relish, pickle juice, eggs, salt, and pepper. Mix thoroughly.

3. Fold in the potatoes, cover, and refrigerate until chilled. Before serving, sprinkle with paprika.

SERVES 6 to 8

Apple Coleslaw

2 raw apples, cored
Juice of 1 lemon
1 (4-ounce) can mandarin oranges, drained and juice reserved
⅓ cup salted peanuts
2 tablespoons sliced green onion (scallion)
2 cups finely shredded green cabbage
⅓ cup French dressing

Slice the unpeeled apples into thin wedges and sprinkle with lemon juice. Place the apples in a salad bowl with the oranges, half the reserved mandarin juice, the peanuts, onion, and cabbage. Toss until well mixed. Before serving, pour the dressing over the salad and toss.

SERVES 4

Callaloo Soup

4 tablespoons (½ stick) butter or margarine
1 medium onion, chopped (about ¾ cup)
1 clove garlic, minced
¾ pound fresh spinach, rinsed and stems removed
3 cups chicken broth
½ cup canned coconut milk
1 medium potato, peeled and diced
1 teaspoon salt
1½ teaspoons ground black pepper
½ pound cooked crabmeat (fresh, canned, or frozen)
Paprika to garnish

1. Melt the butter over medium heat in a large pot. Add the onion and garlic and sauté until the onion is soft, about 5 minutes. Stir in the spinach and cook for an additional 3 minutes, stirring to evenly cook the spinach. Using tongs, remove the spinach to a platter; cover loosely and let cool.

2. In the same pot, combine the broth, coconut milk, potato, salt, and pepper. Bring to a boil over high heat. Reduce the heat to low and simmer, partially covered, 15 minutes, or until the potatoes are just cooked.

3. Using kitchen shears or a knife, cut the cooked spinach into bite-sized pieces. Return the spinach to the pot and simmer uncovered for 2 minutes. Stir in the crabmeat and continue cooking until heated through, about 5 minutes. Sprinkle with paprika and serve hot.

CALLALOO is the name given to many of the popular green-leafed vegetables that are used in Caribbean cooking. In West African cuisine, greens are a staple food, each variety having a specific name. In Nigeria, the term efo is used to refer to the leaves of any root vegetable; silver beet is the name given to spinach greens throughout Africa.

SERVES 4 to 6

African Seafood Soup

1 pound medium uncooked shrimp

2 (3-pound) live lobsters or 2½ pounds frozen lobster tails (about 4 tails)

16 cups (1 gallon) water

2 tablespoons Old Bay seasoning

8 tablespoons (1 stick) salted butter

12 large mushroom cups, chopped

½ cup sherry

2 medium yellow onions, chopped (about 2 cups)

1 large clove garlic, minced

2 medium green bell peppers, cored, seeded, and chopped (about 2 cups)

1 large jalapeño pepper, seeded and minced (about 2 tablespoons)

3 stalks celery, tops removed, chopped

4 medium tomatoes, chopped

1 pound fresh okra, stems removed, cut in half lengthwise

1 (8-ounce) can tomato sauce

1 teaspoon soy sauce

1½ teaspoons Worcestershire sauce

½ teaspoon garlic powder

½ teaspoon ground black pepper

1 teaspoon filé powder

1. Shell and devein the shrimp, reserving the shells and leaving the tails intact. Rinse the lobsters, shrimp, and shrimp shells under cold running water; set aside.

2. In a large pot, bring 1 gallon of water to a boil with the Old Bay seasoning. Add the shrimp to the boiling water and cook about 2 minutes, until the shrimp turn completely pink. Using a strainer, lift the cooked shrimp out of the boiling water and onto a plate. Cover and set aside.

3. Drop the lobsters, head first, into the same pot as the shrimp, making sure the water is rapidly boiling. Cook about 12 to 15 minutes or until

the lobsters turn completely red. Using tongs, carefully lift the lobsters out of the water and onto a cutting board. Let cool.

4. Meanwhile, add the shrimp shells to the boiling water and cook uncovered until reduced by more than half. Using the strainer, lift the shrimp shells out of the water and discard. Reserve the seasoned cooking liquid.

5. In a skillet, melt 4 tablespoons of the butter over medium-high heat. Add the mushrooms and garlic. Sauté about 10 minutes, stirring frequently, until the mushrooms are golden. Stir in ¼ cup of the sherry and cook uncovered 3 minutes to deglaze the pan. Remove the skillet from the heat and set aside to cool.

6. Melt the remaining 4 tablespoons of butter in a separate pot over medium heat. Add the onions and garlic and sauté 3 minutes or until softened. Stir in the bell pepper, jalapeño pepper, and celery. Continue cooking for about 5 minutes, stirring occasionally. Stir in the tomatoes and okra. Increase the heat to medium-high, cover, and cook until the tomatoes have softened and released their juices.

7. Stir the tomato sauce and 6 cups of the reserved cooking liquid into the sautéed vegetable mixture. Add the remaining ¼ cup of sherry, the soy sauce, Worcestershire, garlic powder, black pepper, and filé. Adjust seasoning to taste. Cook uncovered over medium heat for about 30 minutes, stirring occasionally.

8. Meanwhile, remove the lobster meat from the tails and claws. Slice into bite-size pieces. Ten minutes before serving, reheat the soup to a rapid simmer. Stir in the lobster slices, cooked shrimp, and the mushroom-sherry mixture. Cook until heated through, about 5 minutes. Serve immediately.

(continues on next page)

(continued from previous page)

HINT: If using frozen lobster tails, allow the tails to cook only long enough to get thoroughly warm. Do not overcook or the meat will toughen.

FILÉ POWDER is an essential ingredient of the Louisiana Creole kitchen, used to thicken and flavor soups, stews, and gumbos. Filé powder is made from the leaves of the sassafras tree and can be found in the spice section of major supermarkets.

SERVING SUGGESTION: Serve African Seafood Soup over Boiled White Rice (see page 121) with garlic bread and a Sweet Pepper Salad (see page 39).

SERVES 4 TO 6

Buttermilk Biscuits

3 cups all-purpose flour
½ teaspoon salt
½ teaspoon baking soda
1 tablespoon baking powder
½ cup lard or solid vegetable shortening
1 ¼ cups buttermilk

1. Preheat the oven to 425°F. In a mixing bowl, sift together the flour, salt, baking soda, and baking powder. Using a pastry cutter or 2 knives, blend the lard into the dry ingredients until it is evenly dispersed and the size of small coarse beads. Slowly add the buttermilk while stirring with a fork until a moistened dough has formed. Do not overmix.

2. Gently gather the dough into a ball and place it on a floured board. Roll or pat it out to a ¾-inch thickness and cut out biscuits of the desired size. Place side by side on a greased baking sheet. Bake for 15 minutes, until golden.

MAKES 10 TO 12 BISCUITS

Corn Bread

4 tablespoons (½ stick) unsalted butter, melted
1 cup yellow cornmeal
¾ cup all-purpose flour
2 tablespoons granulated sugar
1 tablespoon plus 1 teaspoon baking powder
½ teaspoon salt
1 cup milk
1 large egg, well beaten

1. Preheat the oven to 450°F. Pour 2 tablespoons of the melted butter into a 9-inch baking pan or cast-iron skillet and place in the oven for 5 minutes or until the pan is hot.

2. In a medium bowl, mix together the cornmeal, flour, sugar, baking powder, and salt. Make a well in the center of this mixture and slowly pour in the milk, beating constantly with a wooden spoon to prevent lumps from forming. Mix in the remaining 2 tablespoons of butter and the egg, stirring until completely blended.

3. Pour the batter into the hot pan and bake for 30 to 35 minutes or until the corn bread is golden brown and a toothpick inserted off center comes out clean. Place the corn bread on a baker's rack and let cool in the pan for 15 minutes before serving.

MAKES ONE 9-INCH CORN BREAD

Sweet Potato Corn Bread

1 pound sweet potatoes, peeled and cut into chunks
1 cup buttermilk
1 egg, lightly beaten
1 cup yellow cornmeal
3 tablespoons all-purpose flour
4½ teaspoons baking powder
1 teaspoon salt
1 scant teaspoon baking soda
¼ teaspoon ground allspice
⅛ teaspoon ground cinnamon
3 tablespoons unsalted butter

1. Preheat the oven to 400°F. Combine the potatoes in a saucepan with water to barely cover. Bring to a gentle boil and cook until just tender, about 15 to 20 minutes. Thoroughly drain and pass through a ricer or a wire mesh sieve into a bowl. Add the buttermilk and egg and beat until blended. Set aside.

2. In a mixing bowl, stir together the cornmeal, flour, baking powder, salt, baking soda, allspice, and cinnamon.

3. Put the butter in a 9-inch square baking pan or a 10-inch heavy skillet and place in the preheated oven until melted. Meanwhile, add the dry ingredients to the buttermilk mixture and stir just until blended. Immediately pour the batter into the heated baking pan. Bake about 25 minutes or until the bread is lightly golden and has released from the edges of the pan. Remove from the oven and let cool 5 minutes before serving.

MAKES 6 SERVINGS

Hominy Spoon Bread

AFRICAN
AMERICAN

½ cup regular or quick-cooking hominy grits
2½ cups water
2 tablespoons butter plus additional for serving
3 eggs, separated
½ cup white cornmeal
2 teaspoons baking powder
½ teaspoon salt

1. Cook the grits with the water according to package directions. Stir in the butter and let cool for 5 minutes. Beat the egg yolks into the grits mixture until creamy and well blended. Cover and set aside.

2. In a mixing bowl, stir together the cornmeal, baking powder, and salt; blend into the grits mixture. In a separate bowl, beat the egg whites until they form soft peaks. Using a spatula or wooden spoon, fold the beaten egg whites into the grits mixture.

3. Pour the batter into a buttered ovenproof casserole. Bake in a preheated 350°F oven for 1 hour or until golden brown. Serve hot with butter, if desired.

SERVES 4

Chapatis (Flat Bread)

3 cups unbleached all-purpose flour plus additional for dusting
½ teaspoon salt
½ cup vegetable oil plus additional for frying
6 to 8 tablespoons water

1. Combine 3 cups of flour and the salt in a large bowl. Stir in ½ cup of oil, mixing well. Add between 6 and 8 tablespoons of water, 2 tablespoons at a time, stirring after each addition until the dough holds a shape but is still soft. Knead the dough in the bowl until smooth. Pinch off 12 equal-size pieces, roll into balls, and cover with a damp cloth.

2. Sprinkle about 2 tablespoons of flour on a cutting board or flat surface. Take a 2-inch ball of dough and roll it over to a ⅛-inch-thick round, about the size of a saucer. Repeat with the remaining dough, using additional flour to dust the board.

3. In a heavy skillet, heat 1 tablespoon of oil over medium-high heat until hot. Fry the chapatis, one at a time, for 3 to 5 minutes per side until golden, turning once. As a chapati is done, remove it from the frying pan onto absorbent towels, covering to keep warm. Repeat the process with the remaining chapatis. Serve hot.

MAKES 12

Kuli-Kuli (Groundnut Flat Cakes)

2 pounds salted groundnuts (peanuts)
⅓ cup hot water
Peanut oil for deep-frying

1. Place the groundnuts in a food processor bowl or blender container; grind until pulverized.

2. While the processor is running, drizzle in up to ⅓ cup of hot water in order to extract as much peanut oil as possible. Place the groundnut mixture in a mixing bowl. Using your hands, squeeze and knead the mixture until soft and pliable. At this point, the mixture should resemble a coarse dough that can be gathered into a ball without crumbling. If not, knead 1 to 2 tablespoons of peanut oil into the mixture until the desired consistency is achieved.

3. Divide the dough into 12 equal portions. Place each portion between the palms of your hands and squeeze out as much oil as possible. Shape into flat cakes; cover and set aside.

4. In a deep fryer or heavy skillet, heat sufficient oil for frying to 380°F. Place the groundnut cakes, 2 or 3 at a time, in the hot oil. Fry, turning once, until golden. Remove kuli-kuli from the oil and drain on absorbent towels.

SERVING SUGGESTION: Serve the groundnut cakes with stews, sauces, and soups; or crumble over boiled yams, cassava, and plantains. Once cool, the groundnut cakes can be kept in an airtight container for up to 1 week.

MAKES 12 FLAT CAKES

Koliko (Taro Chips)

4 large (taro) frying cocoyams (about 1 pound)
Oil for deep-frying
Salt
Finely chopped cilantro

Peel the taro and place in water to prevent discoloration. Using a sharp knife or the thin slicing blade of a food processor, slice widthwise into chips. In a large heavy skillet, heat sufficient oil for deep frying. Dry the taro slices thoroughly with kitchen toweling and generously sprinkle with salt. In small batches, fry the chips until golden and crisp, being careful not to burn them. Place the taro chips on absorbent towels to drain off excess oil. Serve immediately.

SERVES 4

FAMILY

Mildred's Aunt Elsie and her mother looked so much alike that people often confused them. Mildred got angry with her mother once because she had called out to her on the street and her mother seemed to ignore her. Imagine her confusion when she found out she had mistaken her Aunt Elsie for her mother! Aunt Elsie was a wonder . . . she was sweet, very loving, and always had something good to say about everyone. The only thing she *wasn't* was really an aunt. The day Mildred mistook her for her mother was the day Elsie and Mildred's mother became friends for life. Within our culture, the family is an extended unit . . . friends, relatives, neighbors . . . together making a family that can meet any challenge. Life's first lessons are taught within the protective and loving circle of the family. Mother, father, sister, brother, aunt, uncle, cousin . . . members can be born into this unit and share a blood tie, or can claim one another and share a love tie. No matter how they come to join the family, the tie that binds is as delicious as Aunt Elsie's treasured gumbo recipe. It is as hearty as groundnut stew and as fulfilling as roasted yams after a long fast.

CHAPTER FIVE

Hearty Stews

West African cuisine includes an assortment of
lavishly seasoned, very hot and spicy stews,
referred to as soups, gravies, and sauces. In
these intricate dishes, meat and fish are treated
as a flavoring rather than the main ingredient,
yielding luscious thick sauces produced by the
slow cooking of indigenous vegetables. Okra,
greens, and eggplant are simmered with meats
until they actually disintegrate. Chile peppers
account for the hot accent, and exotic spices
such as ginger, allspice, and curry produce a
fragrant, rich, spicy vegetable-meat sauce. Served
with simple vegetables, rice, porridges, or
dumplings, these stews form the heart of the
cuisine. West African groundnut stews are
known throughout Africa. Peanuts, imported
from the New World, are ground andused as
thickening agents alongside tomatoes, onion, and
of course chile peppers. These creamy, rich
peanut sauces are served with chicken, seafood,
and vegetables, depending on the occasion.

Liberian-Style Fish Gravy

8 bone-in red snapper steaks (about 1 ½ pounds)
1 teaspoon salt
1 teaspoon ground black pepper
4 cloves garlic, pressed
1 teaspoon red chili powder or ground red pepper (cayenne)
4 large onions, divided (2 onions quartered, 2 onions chopped)
2 large beefsteak tomatoes, cut up
1 fresh red chile pepper or ½ sweet red bell pepper
1 ½ tablespoons Mixed Spice (see page 164)
Peanut oil for frying
1 (6-ounce) can tomato paste
1 ½ cups water
½ bunch chopped fresh basil (about ½ cup packed)
½ teaspoon dried oregano, crushed
2 fish- or chicken-flavored bouillon cubes

1. Rinse the fish steaks under cold running water and pat dry. With a mortar and pestle, grind together the salt, black pepper, garlic, and chili powder. Rub the paste into both sides of the fish steaks. Place in a rectangular baking dish, cover with plastic wrap, and refrigerate for 30 minutes.

2. Meanwhile, combine the quartered onions, tomatoes, chile pepper (or bell pepper), and 1 tablespoon of the mixed spice in a blender. Purée until smooth, adding a little water if necessary. Set aside.

3. In a skillet large enough to hold the fish steaks in a single layer, warm 3 or 4 tablespoons of oil over medium heat. Fry the fish steaks, turning once, until crisp but not blackened, 2 to 4 minutes on each side. Remove the steaks with a slotted spatula and cover to keep warm. Set aside.

4. In the same skillet, warm 1 cup of the peanut oil over medium heat. Carefully pour in the puréed onion mixture and the tomato paste; fry

for 3 minutes, stirring constantly. Add the 1½ cups of water, the basil, oregano, bouillon cubes, and the remaining ½ tablespoon of mixed spice. Stir and bring to a boil over medium heat. Adjust the sauce for seasoning.

LIBERIA

5. Remove the bones from the fish steaks. Place the steaks in the sauce and add the chopped onions. Continue cooking over medium heat until the sauce is reduced by half. The sauce should not be pourable, but rather thick and spoonable, and the fish should flake coarsely but not disintegrate.

SERVING SUGGESTION: Serve Liberian-Style Fish Gravy over Boiled White Rice (see page 121) or with Black-Eyed Peas and Ham Hocks (see page 130). Accompany with boiled cassava, plantains, or sweet potatoes.

SERVES 6

Chicken Groundnut Stew with Vegetables

CHICKEN
4 chicken hindquarters (legs and thighs) or 1 (3-pound) guinea fowl
8 cloves garlic
1 tablespoon ground thyme
3 tablespoons lemon juice
1 teaspoon salt
⅓ cup palm or vegetable oil for pan-frying

GROUNDNUT (PEANUT) STEW
1 yellow onion, finely chopped
3 tablespoons tomato paste
1 (14¼-ounce) can whole tomatoes and juice, blended (about 1¾ cups)
¼ teaspoon dark Nigerian chili powder or ground red pepper (cayenne)
⅓ cup ground roasted peanuts (groundnuts) or natural peanut butter
3 cups well-seasoned chicken broth
2 soft-cooked eggs, peeled
¾ cup sliced okra
¾ cup diced yams
¾ cup cut green beans
Plantain Fufu (see page 136) or Banku (Commeal Dumplings, see page 141)

GARNISHES
Shredded coconut
Pineapple chunks
Raisins
Sliced green and red bell peppers
Mandarin orange segments
Kuli-Kuli (see page 54) (optional)

1. Rinse the chicken pieces under cold running water; pat dry and place in a shallow dish. In a mortar or bowl, grind the garlic, thyme, lemon juice, and salt into a paste. Rub half the paste into the chicken until well coated. Cover and refrigerate 1 hour.

2. Warm the oil in a frying pan over medium-high heat. Place the chicken pieces in the hot oil and fry, turning occasionally, until golden, about 15 minutes. Remove the chicken from the pan and cover to keep warm. Leave the oil and chicken juices in the skillet.

3. Sauté the onion over medium heat in the same skillet used for frying the chicken, stirring to loosen the fried bits that have stuck to the bottom of the skillet. Add the tomato paste, the remaining garlic paste, the blended tomatoes, and the chili powder. Cook over medium heat, stirring frequently, until the tomato juices have reduced. Whisk the groundnuts into the tomato sauce until creamy and smooth. Slowly whisk in the chicken broth and cook for 10 minutes over medium-low heat, stirring occasionally to prevent the groundnuts from sticking. If desired, remove any excess oil that has accumulated on top of the stew.

4. Place the chicken pieces into the sauce. Cover and simmer gently for 15 minutes, occasionally turning the chicken. When the chicken is cooked and has absorbed the flavors of the sauce, drop the 2 cooked eggs into the stew along with the raw vegetables. Continue to cook for 15 minutes, adding additional broth as needed to maintain a thick stew-like consistency.

5. Place some plantain fufu (stiff porridge) or dumplings (banku) in shallow bowls. Top with the groundnut sauce, chicken, and vegetables. Offer small bowls of the shredded fresh coconut, pineapple chunks, raisins, sliced peppers, mandarin orange segments, and kuli-kuli to garnish the stew.

SERVES 4 TO 6

Chicken Groundnut Soup—the Ghanaian Way

1 broiler/fryer chicken, about 3 to 3½ pounds, cut into serving pieces
1 large oval eggplant or 6 Japanese eggplants, peeled and cubed (about 6 cups)
3½ cups water
1 extra-large chicken-flavored bouillon cube
1 (2-inch) piece fresh ginger, peeled and sliced
1 teaspoon salt
1 cup groundnut (peanut) paste or smooth peanut butter
1 tablespoon tomato paste
1 medium white onion, chopped (about 1 cup)
1 (14½-ounce) can whole tomatoes and juice, blended
1 teaspoon ground ginger
1 teaspoon grated nutmeg
3 cloves garlic, minced
1 large red bell pepper, cored, seeded, and cut up
3 red jalapeño chile peppers, stems removed, seeded, and halved

1. In a small pot, combine the chicken and eggplant with 3 cups of the water, the bouillon cube, sliced ginger, and salt. Bring to a boil; cover the pot and reduce the heat. Simmer over very low heat for 20 minutes or until the chicken is just cooked. Remove the eggplant to a bowl; cover and set aside. Pull the meat from the chicken, reserve the broth, and discard the bones. (Makes 2 cups broth and 3 cups pulled chicken.)

2. Meanwhile, in a second pot, mix the groundnut paste with the remaining ½ cup of water. Cook over medium heat, stirring constantly, until the oil has separated from the paste. Mix in the tomato paste until smooth. Lower the heat and fry about 5 minutes. Stir in the onion, tomatoes, ginger, nutmeg, and garlic. Continue cooking over low heat, stirring frequently, until the onion has softened. Add the cooked chicken pieces and 1 cup of the chicken broth. Mix well and bring to a boil. Lower the heat and simmer covered for 10 minutes.

3. In a blender container, purée the cooked eggplant, the remaining cup of chicken broth, the bell pepper, and jalapeño peppers until smooth. Strain and add to the stew. Mix well and adjust the seasoning to taste. Bring to a boil and cook covered for 20 minutes.

SERVING SUGGESTION: Serve hot with coarsely chopped roasted groundnuts and Boiled White Rice (see page 121) or yams.

GROUNDNUT PASTE: Roast 2 cups of shelled peanuts in a preheated 375°F oven until brown. Remove the skins and grind the roasted peanuts in a coffee or meat grinder. Add salt to taste. Makes 1½ cups.

GROUNDNUTS, the African name for peanuts, form the base for many of the rich and tantalizing West African one-pot stews.

SERVES 4

Curried Shrimp Groundnut Stew

3 tablespoons palm oil or vegetable oil
3 cloves garlic, minced
1 medium onion, chopped
1½ pounds shrimp, shelled and deveined
2 medium ripe tomatoes, coarsely chopped
1 teaspoon curry powder
½ teaspoon dried thyme leaves, crushed
½ teaspoon ground red pepper (cayenne)
½ cup creamy peanut butter
¼ to ⅓ cup water
Boiled White Rice (see page 121) or Mashed Rice (see page 120)
Chopped cilantro to garnish

1. In a large frying pan, heat the oil over medium heat until it is hot but not smoking. Reduce the heat to medium and add the garlic, onion, and shrimp, stirring for 2 to 3 minutes, until the garlic is golden brown, the shrimp are pink, and the onion is soft.

2. Add the tomatoes, curry powder, thyme, and cayenne to the shrimp mixture. Cook for about 5 minutes, stirring occasionally, until the tomatoes release their juices.

3. In a small bowl, combine the peanut butter and ¼ cup of the water. Stir to make a smooth paste. Slowly add the peanut butter to the stew, stirring until it is well combined. Bring to a boil over medium-high heat, lower the heat, and simmer for 5 minutes. If a thinner consistency is desired, add an additional ¼ cup water to thin or ¼ cup peanut butter to thicken.

4. To serve, place a mound (about ¾ cup) of rice in a shallow bowl. Ladle the stew around the rice and garnish with cilantro.

SERVES 4 TO 6

Game Hens in Smothered Onion Sauce

⅓ cup peanut oil
4 Rock Cornish game hens, halved
Salt and black pepper to taste
4 large onions, chopped (about 6 cups)
1 (6-ounce) can tomato paste
2 cups water
2 fresh bay leaves or 4 dried leaves
1 teaspoon paprika or red chili powder
1 teaspoon dried thyme leaves, crushed
1 extra-large chicken-flavored bouillon cube
Cooked brown rice
Chopped parsley to garnish

1. Warm the oil over medium-high heat in a large frying pan. Season the hens with salt and pepper and brown them on both sides in the hot oil until golden, about 10 minutes. Remove the hens and cover to keep warm.

2. In the same skillet, stir the onions and tomato paste into the warm oil and sauté over medium heat until the onions have softened, about 10 minutes. Add the water, bay leaves, paprika, thyme, and bouillon cube. Mix well and bring to a boil. Add the hens to the sauce; cover and cook for 15 minutes. Uncover, stir, and adjust the seasoning. Continue cooking uncovered until the sauce has reduced. Place the hens on a serving platter accompanied by brown rice. Ladle the onion-tomato sauce over the chicken and rice and garnish with chopped parsley.

SERVING SUGGESTION: Serve with Okro (Fried Okra, see page 147) or sautéed greens.

SERVES 4

Chicken Breast in Okra-Palava Sauce

1 pound (about 3) boneless, skinless chicken breasts
1 ½ teaspoons garlic salt
½ teaspoon ground black pepper
Flour for dusting
⅓ cup red palm oil or peanut oil
1 (16-ounce) package frozen okra, sliced into ½-inch rounds
½ teaspoon dried thyme
1 medium onion, chopped (about 1 cup)
½ cup chicken broth
Boiled White Rice (see page 121)

1. Rinse the chicken breasts under cold running water and pat dry. Cut them into bite-size pieces and season with garlic salt and black pepper. Place the chicken in a sealable plastic bag with sufficient flour for dusting. Seal the bag and shake until the chicken is completely coated. Refrigerate until ready to fry.

2. Heat the palm oil in a frying pan over medium-high heat. Add the chicken pieces and fry, turning as needed, until browned. Lower the heat to medium-low and stir in the okra, thyme, and onion. Sauté until the onion has browned, about 8 to 10 minutes, stirring frequently. Pour in the broth and continue cooking for 5 minutes or until the sauce has thickened. Serve with white rice.

SERVES 4

Chicken in a Spicy Peanut Sauce

1 ½ pounds boneless, skinless chicken breast halves (about 4)
1 teaspoon salt
1 teaspoon ground white pepper
1 ½ teaspoons ground ginger
2 tablespoons peanut oil
2 red jalapeño chile peppers, stemmed, seeded, and slivered (or substitute half
    a red bell pepper)
2 green jalapeño chile peppers, stemmed, seeded, and slivered
2 tablespoons tomato paste
1 cup water
3 tablespoons creamy peanut butter
⅓ cup sliced green onions (scallions)

1. Rinse the chicken under cold running water and pat dry. Cut into bite-size pieces and season with salt, pepper, and ginger; cover and refrigerate until ready to cook.

2. In a skillet, warm the oil over medium-high heat and sauté the chicken with the chile peppers until the chicken has browned. Stir in the tomato paste and water; mix until blended. Whisk in the peanut butter and cook covered, stirring occasionally, for 20 minutes or until the sauce has thickened to the consistency of light cream. Adjust the seasoning to taste and sprinkle with green onions before serving.

SERVES 4

Lamb and Eggplant Sauce

NIGERIA

1 pound boneless lamb, trimmed of fat and cut into small pieces
1 medium onion, halved
1 extra-large beef-flavored bouillon cube
1 teaspoon salt
3 cups water plus additional as needed
⅓ cup groundnut (peanut) oil
1 large onion, chopped (about 1½ cups)
1 large red bell pepper, cored and chopped (about 1½ cups)
1 (14½-ounce) can whole tomatoes and juice, cut up (about 1¾ cups)
4 cups cubed eggplant (about 1 large oval or 4 Japanese eggplants)
2 red jalapeño or serrano chile peppers, seeded and minced
1½ teaspoons ground cumin
½ teaspoon turmeric

1. In a small pot, combine the lamb, onion halves, bouillon cube, and salt with 3 cups of the water or enough to barely cover. Bring to a boil. Lower the heat and cook, partially covered, until the lamb is tender, about 40 minutes, adding additional hot water if necessary. Strain, reserving 2 cups of the broth. Discard the onion.

2. In a 2-quart pot, warm the oil over medium-high heat. Add the chopped onion and sauté for 3 minutes or until softened. Stir in the bell pepper and tomatoes. Continue cooking, stirring occasionally, until the tomato juices begin to evaporate.

3. Add the eggplant, jalapeño pepper, cumin, and turmeric. Return the cooked lamb to the pot, along with the remaining ½ cup water and the 2 cups of reserved cooking liquid. Bring to a boil; reduce the heat to very low and cook covered for 30 minutes. Stir and mash the mixture

every 10 minutes, adding additional water if the sauce becomes too thick. The sauce will have finished cooking when the eggplant has disintegrated, creating a thick but pourable consistency. Skim off the excess oil and discard. Adjust the seasoning to taste and serve hot.

NIGERIA

SERVING SUGGESTION: Serve Yam and Sweet Potato Fufu (see page 137) or Tuwo Ginkafa (Mashed Rice, see page 120).

SERVES 6

Peanut Butter Lamb Soup

NIGERIA,
GHANA,
TOGO,
IVORY
COAST

1 pound boneless lamb, trimmed of fat and diced
1 onion, halved
1 carrot, cut up
1 stalk celery, cut up
2 bay leaves
1 extra-large beef bouillon cube
1 teaspoon dried thyme leaves, crushed
½ teaspoon salt
Water for cooking
1 (14½-ounce) can diced tomatoes and juice
2 (8-ounce) cans tomato sauce
2 tablespoons minced garlic
1 to 2½ cups peanut butter
Coarsely ground peanuts to garnish
Chopped green onions (scallions)

1. In a pot, combine the lamb, onion, carrot, celery, bay leaves, bouillon cube, thyme, and salt. Add water to cover by 2 inches. Bring to a boil, lower the heat, and cook partially covered for 40 minutes or until the meat is tender. With a slotted spoon, remove the meat and discard the onion. If necessary, add water to make 3 cups of stock.

2. Add the tomatoes, tomato sauce, and garlic to the lamb stock. Cook over medium-high heat for 10 minutes. Whisk in 2 cups of the peanut butter until blended. Add the cooked lamb, cover, and let simmer over medium-low heat for 1 hour. Every 10 minutes stir the soup to prevent the peanut butter from settling to the bottom. By the end of the cooking time, the peanut butter will be dissolved. Adjust the seasoning or thickness by adding in the remaining ½ cup of peanut butter if desired. Garnish the soup with ground peanuts and green onions and serve hot.

VARIATION: Substitute chicken for lamb.

SERVES 6 TO 8

Kedienou (Spicy Lamb Gravy)

IVORY
COAST

2 tablespoons butter
1 cup diced yellow onion
1 tablespoon minced serrano chile pepper
3 cloves garlic, minced
2 pounds boneless lamb, cut into chunks
1 teaspoon salt
½ teaspoon ground red pepper (cayenne)
1 teaspoon thyme leaves, crushed (optional)
1 (14½-ounce) can diced tomatoes and juice
2 chicken-flavored bouillon cubes dissolved in ½ cup warm water

Place the butter, onion, chile pepper, and garlic in the bottom of a 3½-
to 6-quart crockery slow cooker. Top with the lamb pieces that have
been seasoned with salt, cayenne, and thyme. Pour the diced tomatoes
(and juice) and dissolved bouillon cubes over the meat pieces. Cover
and cook on the low heat setting for 10 hours or the high heat setting
for 6 hours.

SERVING SUGGESTION: Serve over Boiled White Rice (see page 121)
accompanied by sautéed greens.

SERVES 4

Sidio with Gari (Beef–Peanut Butter Sauce with Cassava Meal)

2 tablespoons butter or oil
1½ pounds lean boneless beef (top round or loin), cut into small pieces or minced
½ cup finely chopped yellow onion
1 tablespoon minced serrano chile pepper
1 teaspoon salt
1 teaspoon ground black pepper
½ cup tomato paste
1 extra-large beef bouillon cube
4 cups water
1¼ to 1¾ cups smooth or crunchy peanut butter
1 cup sliced green onions (both white and green sections)
Gari (see recipe below) or couscous

1. In a skillet, melt the butter over medium-high heat. Add the meat, onion, and chile pepper. Generously season with salt and pepper. Fry, stirring occasionally, until the meat has browned.

2. Add the tomato paste, bouillon cube, and water to the beef; thoroughly mix to dissolve the bouillon cube. Bring to a boil, lower the heat, and simmer covered for 30 minutes or until the meat is tender. Add 1¼ cups of peanut butter and stir until completely blended into the sauce. Adjust the seasoning to taste, adding up to ½ cup more of the peanut butter. Cook over low heat for 15 minutes, stirring occasionally. Serve hot, garnished with green onions and accompanied by gari (cooked cassava meal) or couscous.

VARIATION: Substitute skinless boneless chicken breast, cut into small pieces, for beef.

GARI (FARINA DE MANIOCA) Gari is dried, coarsely ground cassava meal that is toasted, then rehydrated in water to make a grainlike dish resembling couscous. It is used much like rice. To prepare gari, or farina de manioca, place 1 cup of cassava meal in a 3-cup bowl. Stir in enough cold water to completely cover the cassava meal. Let stand for 10 minutes or until the gari absorbs all of the water and swells. Stir the gari with a fork until fluffy. Serve with a hot meat or fish sauce. Makes 2 cups.

IVORY COAST

SERVES 4

Okra Beef Sauce

½ cup palm or peanut oil
1 pound beef clod or stewing beef, cut into small pieces
1 teaspoon salt
1 teaspoon paprika
1 teaspoon ground black pepper
1½ teaspoons ground cumin
1 large onion, cut into 1-inch strips (about 1½ cups)
1 (14½-ounce) can whole tomatoes and juice, cut up (about 1¾ cups)
8 cups water
3 pounds okra, stems removed, rinsed, and cut into ½-inch-thick slices (about 7 to 8 cups)
2 extra-large beef-flavored bouillon cubes
3 hot chile serrano peppers, stems removed, seeded and minced
Chopped cilantro for garnishing

1. In a large pot, combine ¼ cup of the palm oil and beef; generously season to taste with salt, paprika, black pepper, and ½ teaspoon of the cumin. Fry the beef over medium-high heat until seared. Add the onion and continue frying until the onion is browned, about 8 minutes. Stir in the tomatoes and cook, stirring constantly, until the tomato juices begin to evaporate, about 5 minutes.

3. Pour in the water and bring to a boil. Add the remaining ¼ cup of oil and the okra. Return to a boil, lower the heat, and cook uncovered for 40 minutes or until the liquid has reduced by half. Add the bouillon cubes, the remaining 1 teaspoon of cumin, and the minced peppers to the pot. Continue cooking for 10 minutes. Adjust the seasoning to taste. Sprinkle with cilantro before serving.

SERVING SUGGESTION: Accompany with Boiled White Rice (see page 121) and boiled white or yellow sweet potatoes and serve with Red Pepper Dipping Sauce (see page 161).

SERVES 8 TO 10

Black-Eyed Peas in Groundnut Sauce

AFRICAN
AMERICAN

2 tablespoons oil
1 medium onion, sliced into 1-inch-thick strips
1 fresh green Anaheim chile pepper, stemmed, seeded, and chopped (about ⅓ cup)
1 cup canned diced tomatoes or 1 medium ripe tomato, blanched, peeled, and diced
½ cup unsalted peanuts, ground in a spice grinder (about ¾ cup)
2 (16-ounce) cans black-eyed peas, drained and rinsed (about 3 cups)
Salt to season

1. In a heavy pot, warm the oil over medium-high heat. Add the onion and chile pepper and sauté until the onion begins to turn golden brown. Stir in the tomatoes and ground peanuts. Continue cooking, stirring occasionally, for about 5 minutes.

2. Add the black-eyed peas and 1 cup of water to the pot. Bring to a boil, lower the heat, and simmer covered for 30 minutes, stirring occasionally.

3. Serve with Boiled White Rice (see page 121) and spicy Steamed Spinach with Okra (see page 146).

MAKES 4½ CUPS

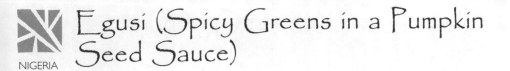

Egusi (Spicy Greens in a Pumpkin Seed Sauce)

NIGERIA

1 pound boneless beef or mutton, cut into bite-size chunks
1 medium onion, halved
Salt
1 cup egusi (pumpkin seeds) (see below)
1 tablespoon iru (vegetable–locust bean seasoning), or 1 extra-large vegetable-flavored bouillon cube (see below)
1 tablespoon minced red chile pepper or 1 teaspoon ground red pepper (cayenne)
1 bunch purslane (verdolagas), kale, or turnip greens
½ cup palm oil or peanut oil
1 small onion, sliced into 1-inch strips
⅓ cup tomato paste
1 tablespoon cider vinegar
1 tablespoon shrimp powder or ground dried shrimps (optional)

1. In a small pot, combine the beef with one of the onion halves, 1 teaspoon of salt, and water to cover by 2 inches. Bring to a boil, lower the heat, and cook partially covered until tender, about 45 minutes. Strain, reserving the broth.

2. Meanwhile, dissolve the iru or the bouillon cube in ½ cup of water. Grind the pumpkin seeds until pulverized and place in blender with the dissolved bouillon, the remaining onion half, and the chile pepper. Blend until smooth and set the purée aside.

3. Rinse the greens under cold running water to remove loose dirt; slice off the stems. In a saucepan, bring 4 cups of water and 1 teaspoon of salt to a rapid boil. Add the leaves and cook uncovered for 5 minutes. Immediately drain and rinse the leaves under cold running water. Place the greens on a cutting board and chop into small pieces; set aside.

4. In a separate pot, warm the palm oil over medium-high heat. Carefully (to avoid splashing the hot fat) add the cooked beef and onion. Quickly fry until the beef is browned. Stir in the tomato paste blended with the seasoning purée and bring to a boil. Cook for 3 minutes, stirring constantly. Pour in 2 cups of reserved beef broth. Lower the heat and simmer uncovered for 10 minutes.

NIGERIA

5. Add the chopped greens, vinegar, and shrimp powder (if desired). Stir to mix thoroughly. Adjust the seasoning to taste and cook over medium-low heat until the sauce has thickened, about 15 minutes.

SERVING SUGGESTION: Serve egusi with a yam fufu (see page 137) and Gari (see page 73).

VARIATION: Add 2 cups of sliced fresh okra with the greens for an especially delicious stew.

EFO is the West African name given to greens.

EGUSI is the seed of the African egusi squash. Ground egusi seeds are used to thicken and flavor soup; their use is similar to that of pumpkin seeds. You can substitute hulled pumpkin seeds pulverized in a spice grinder or use ½ cup tapioca flour dissolved in warm broth.

IRU is a vegetable seasoning made from the bean of the African locust tree, not to be confused with the locust tree of the Mediterranean.

SERVES 4 TO 6

Vegetables in a Groundnut Sauce

SAUCE

4½ cups water

⅓ cup plus 1 tablespoon natural peanut butter

2 tablespoons groundnut (peanut) oil

1 cup finely chopped yellow onion

½ cup each finely chopped green and red bell pepper

1 hot chile pepper, minced

1 teaspoon red chili powder or paprika

½ teaspoon ground allspice

½ teaspoon dried thyme leaves, crushed

2 tablespoons tomato paste

1 vegetable- or chicken-flavored bouillon cube

VEGETABLES

½ cup vegetable oil

2 yellow plantains, peeled and diced (about 2 cups)

4 tablespoons (½ stick) butter

2 carrots, peeled and sliced (about 1 cup)

½ cup green beans, in 1-inch pieces

½ cup frozen lima beans, thawed

½ cup frozen peas, thawed

3 stalks green onion, minced (about 1 cup)

Steamed white or brown rice

1. In a small saucepan, heat ½ cup of the water to boiling. Stir in the peanut butter until dissolved. Cook over medium-high heat, stirring frequently to prevent sticking, for about 5 minutes. Remove the peanut sauce from the heat, cover, and keep warm.

2. In a skillet, heat the oil and sauté the onion, bell peppers, and chile pepper over medium-high heat, stirring occasionally, until the onion has softened. Stir in the chili powder, allspice, and thyme. Cook for 1 minute. Add the remaining 4 cups of water, the tomato paste, bouillon cube, and the peanut sauce. Stir to combine and simmer uncovered for

20 minutes or until the sauce has thickened to the consistency of heavy cream. Adjust the seasoning to taste, remove from the heat, and cover the sauce to keep warm. Makes 3½ cups.

IVORY COAST

3. While the sauce is cooking, prepare the vegetables. Heat the oil over medium-high heat in a large skillet. Add the plantains and pan-fry until golden and soft when pierced with fork. Remove from the skillet and place on absorbent towels to drain excess oil.

4. In the same skillet, melt the butter over medium heat. Add the carrots, green beans, and lima beans. Sauté for 10 minutes or until just soft, stirring occasionally. Mix in the peas and cooked plantains, cooking and occasionally stirring until the vegetables are thoroughly heated. Pour the sauce over the vegetables, mix well, and garnish with the green onions. Serve immediately accompanied by Boiled White Rice (see page 121).

SERVES 6

Kontomiré Stew (Spinach Leaf Sauce)

5 cups (1½ pounds) kontomiré or substitute spinach, Swiss chard, or mustard greens, rinsed and trimmed
⅓ cup palm oil or corn oil mixed with 1 tablespoon ground turmeric
1 large onion, chopped (about 1½ cups)
2 ripe tomatoes, chopped (about 1 cup)
2 fresh chile peppers, finely chopped, or ½ teaspoon red chili powder
¾ cup water
12 canned anchovy fillets, drained and mashed
4 hard-cooked eggs, halved
⅓ cup shelled pumpkin seeds, ground
Cooked rice, boiled or roasted yams, or Banku (Cornmeal Dumplings, see page 141)

1. In a stockpot, heat 3 quarts of water to boiling. Drop the greens into the water, return to a boil, and cook uncovered for 1 minute. Drain immediately. Chop the leaves and set aside.

2. Warm the oil in a large skillet over medium-high heat. Add the onion, tomatoes, and chile peppers. Sauté, stirring frequently, for about 3 minutes. Pour in the ¾ cup of water and simmer uncovered for 5 minutes. Add the chopped greens and anchovies. Continue cooking while stirring and mashing the greens until the sauce has thickened, about 20 minutes. (Do not boil the mixture or the greens will turn bitter.) Season to taste with additional chili peppers or anchovies. To serve, pour the sauce over egg halves and sprinkle with ground pumpkin seeds. Accompany with rice, yams, or Banku.

VARIATION: To prepare this dish in the style of Sierra Leone, add 1 pound of shelled fresh shrimp for the last 7 minutes of cooking. Generously top with groundnuts (chopped peanuts).

SERVES 4

Oxtail Stew

2 pounds oxtail, trimmed of excess fat and cut into 1½-inch chunks
1 teaspoon salt
¼ teaspoon pepper
1 (14½-ounce) can tomatoes
1 medium onion, chopped
1 green bell pepper, chopped
2 carrots, peeled and sliced ½ inch thick
2 cups shredded cabbage
½ cup uncooked rice
2 medium potatoes, peeled and diced
½ teaspoon celery seed
½ teaspoon dried red pepper flakes, or to taste
¾ pound fresh okra, trimmed and cut into ½-inch chunks, or 1 (10-ounce) package frozen okra, thawed

1. Rinse the oxtail, place in a large kettle or stockpot, and add cold water to cover. Season with salt and pepper, bring to a boil, and reduce the heat. Cover and simmer until the meat is fork-tender, about 3 hours.

2. Cool the broth and refrigerate overnight if time permits, so the fat will harden and can be removed easily. Or skim off as much fat as possible from the warm broth.

3. Add the tomatoes with their juice, the onion, green pepper, carrots, cabbage, rice, potatoes, and seasonings. Cover and simmer until the vegetables are tender, about 20 minutes. Taste and adjust the seasoning.

4. Add the okra and simmer 5 minutes longer. Serve with Boiled White Rice (see page 121).

SERVES 8

DIGNITY

A news segment on television one evening concerned victim relief for a small African country. Although the content of the story was quite sad, the images of the people were remarkable. The women were caring for their children as best they could with pride and love. The men were using all their energy to eke out a way to keep their families together; their faces showed a firm resolve to overcome their troubles. Dignity was personified in that news story. When the world seems to be crashing down all around you and you can still walk with your head held high, that is dignity. When you seem to make mistakes at every turn, and try as you might to right the wrongs that seem unrightable, and you can still smile, that is dignity. When a people can come through the fire and still seek the flame of hope, that is dignity. The dignity of a people is rooted in self-love and self-knowledge. Its authenticity is rooted in a people's sense of identity, and that authenticity is re-flected in their creativity. Nowhere is our creativity more evident than in our culinary arts. A people who truly know themselves are free to create that which expresses that collective identity. Where else but from dignity could a really good jambalaya spring?

CHAPTER SIX

Fish, Seafood, Poultry, and Meat Entrees

West Africa's coastline provides an
abundance of fish and shellfish, holding a
prominent role in coastal cuisine.
Throughout the countryside, meat is
scarce and used in small portions.
Chicken tends to be the special-
occasion food. All of these entree dishes
are fragrantly seasoned with chile, fresh
ginger, and aromatic spices as is the
tradition of Caribbean and African
American cooks. Fresh fish and seafood,
caught daily along the coast, are served
in a variety of ways—smoked, stuffed,
grilled, and battered and fried.

Ginger-Roasted Fish

1 (3- to 4-pound) rockfish, mullet, or snapper
1 (3-ounce) piece gingerroot, peeled and grated (about ¼ cup)
3 fresh hot chile peppers, minced (jalapeño, serrano, or cayenne Tabasco)
3 large cloves garlic
2 teaspoons salt
2 tablespoons vegetable oil, plus additional for frying
Spinach leaves, washed and stemmed
Thinly sliced red bell peppers and red onion for garnish

1. Scale and rinse the fish; place on a cutting board and make 4 or 5 deep but short diagonal cuts 1½ inches apart on each side.

2. Prepare a seasoning paste by grinding the ginger, hot peppers, garlic, and salt in a mortar and pestle until smooth. Stuff the paste in the slits on both sides of the fish. Mix the remaining paste with 2 tablespoons of oil and rub over the fish. Place on a tray; cover with plastic wrap and marinate for several hours in the refrigerator.

3. Preheat the oven to 425°F. Place the fish upright on a poultry roasting rack, or use crumpled foil to support it on both sides and keep the fish upright. Roast for 25 to 40 minutes (depending on size), until the skin is crisp and golden.

SERVING SUGGESTION: Serve hot on a bed of fresh spinach garnished with sweet red bell peppers and onions. Accompany with Sweet Pepper Salad (see page 39), boiled yams (see page 137), and Chile Sambal (see page 159).

FRESH CHILE PEPPERS are an important seasoning in West African cuisine. The closest alternative to these small peppers, known as Nigerian peppers, is a red or yellow Scotch bonnet pepper, a red chile serrano, red cayenne Tabasco, or jalapeño chile pepper.

SERVES 6

Lemon Rice–Stuffed Catfish

AFRICAN
AMERICAN

3 tablespoons butter
⅓ cup sliced celery
2 tablespoons thinly sliced green onion (about 2 stalks)
2 cups cooked brown rice
1 tablespoon grated lemon rind
½ teaspoon salt
½ teaspoon dried thyme
¼ teaspoon ground black pepper
3 tablespoons fresh lemon juice
2 pounds fresh or frozen catfish fillets (about 4 fillets)
Paprika for garnish

1. Preheat the oven to 350°F. In a medium skillet, melt the butter over medium heat. Remove and reserve 1 tablespoon. Sauté the celery and onion in the remaining butter until tender. Stir in the cooked rice, lemon rind, salt, thyme, black pepper, and lemon juice. Mix well, cover, and set aside.

2. Lightly spray a shallow baking dish with vegetable oil cooking spray. Put the fillets on a work surface and spoon the rice mixture over the lower half of each fillet. Roll the fillets lengthwise to enclose the rice mixture and secure each pinwheel with wooden picks. Arrange in the prepared baking dish.

3. Brush each pinwheel with the remaining butter and sprinkle with paprika. Bake uncovered for 20 to 30 minutes (depending on the thickness of the fillet), until the thickest portion of the fillet is opaque.

SERVES 4

Fried Catfish

2 catfish fillets (about 1 pound) cut diagonally into 1 ½-inch pieces
1 teaspoon salt
1 teaspoon ground black pepper
½ teaspoon garlic salt
½ teaspoon onion salt
1 teaspoon paprika or chili powder
1 cup cornmeal
Peanut oil for deep-frying
Lemon wedges for garnish

1. Rinse the fillets under cold running water and pat dry. In a shallow bowl, combine the salt, black pepper, garlic salt, onion salt, paprika, and cornmeal until evenly blended. Press the fillets into the seasonings until well coated on both sides. Place on a platter and refrigerate for 10 minutes, allowing the coating to set.

2. Meanwhile, fill a heavy pot no more than halfway full with peanut oil and heat to 380°F. Working in batches, submerge fillets in the hot oil and fry just until golden and crisp. Serve with lemon wedges.

SERVES 2 TO 4

Crisp Oven-Baked Catfish

AFRICAN
AMERICAN

6 catfish fillets (about 8 ounces each)
Salt and ground pepper to taste
2 cups seasoned cornmeal mix or 2 cups cornmeal mixed with 1 tablespoon
   Mixed Spice (see page 164)
½ teaspoon garlic powder
¼ to ½ teaspoon ground red pepper (cayenne) or 1 teaspoon paprika
4 eggs
Lemon wedges

1. Under cold running water, rinse the catfish fillets; pat dry. Sprinkle each fillet with salt and pepper to season. Cover and refrigerate until ready to bake.

2. Preheat the oven to 375°F. In a medium bowl, mix together the seasoned cornmeal, garlic powder, and cayenne pepper. In a separate bowl, beat the eggs until frothy.

3. Dip one catfish fillet into the beaten egg until completely covered. Lift and quickly place in the cornmeal mixture, covering and pressing the cornmeal into the fillet until well coated on both sides. Using a spatula, place the fillet in a heavy ovenproof skillet that has been coated with vegetable oil cooking spray. Repeat the process with the remaining fillets.

4. Place the skillet in the preheated oven and bake for 25 to 35 minutes depending on the thickness of the fillets. Turn the fillets and continue baking 5 minutes or longer, until completely golden brown and crisp. Serve immediately, garnished with lemon wedges.

SERVES 6

Tuna Poché in a Tomato Case

TUNA POCHÉ
1½ pounds fresh tuna, cut into chunks
Juice of 1 lemon
1 teaspoon salt
½ teaspoon ground white pepper
3 cloves garlic, minced
1 (3-ounce) piece gingerroot, peeled and grated (about ¼ cup)
1 red jalapeño chile pepper, seeded and minced (about 1 tablespoon)
1 cup minced shallots or scallions
¾ cup minced sweet red bell pepper or hot pepper

TOMATO CASE
4 large beefsteak tomatoes, blanched and peeled
Salt to season
Taro Chips (see page 55)
Finely chopped cilantro

1. To poach the tuna: In a 1-quart saucepan, combine the tuna pieces, lemon juice, salt, white pepper, garlic, ginger, and chile pepper with water to barely cover. Bring to a boil, reduce the heat, and simmer, partially covered, for 15 minutes or until the fish just turns opaque in the center. With a slotted spoon, transfer the fish to a bowl, reserving the cooking liquid.

2. Using two forks, flake the fish into small pieces. Stir in 2 to 3 tablespoons of the cooking liquid, the shallots, the bell pepper and mix well. Adjust the seasoning to taste, cover, and set aside. Strain remaining cooking broth, pour it into a gravy bowl, and cover to keep warm.

3. To make the tomato cases: Slice off the upper quarter sections of the whole tomatoes. Carefully scoop out the pulp and seeds, and sprinkle the cavities with salt. Fill each tomato shell with the tuna poché.

SERVES 4

Skillet Turkey Hash

AFRICAN
AMERICAN

3 tablespoons butter
1 medium onion, chopped (about 1 cup)
1 small red bell pepper, cored and chopped (about 1 cup)
8 ounces fresh mushrooms, thickly sliced
2 cloves garlic, minced
4 cups diced cooked turkey
3 cups leftover turkey stuffing or prepared packaged stuffing
¾ cup heavy cream
½ cup turkey gravy
⅓ cup chopped parsley, plus additional for garnish
½ teaspoon grated nutmeg
Salt and ground black pepper

1. Melt the butter in a large, heavy skillet over medium heat. Add the onion and bell pepper and sauté until softened, about 5 minutes. Stir in the mushrooms and garlic and continue sautéing until the mushrooms are soft. Mix in the turkey and stuffing and continue cooking and stirring until heated through, about 5 minutes.

2. Stir in ½ cup of the cream, the gravy, ⅓ cup of parsley, and the nutmeg. Season to taste with salt and black pepper. Cook over medium-high heat, shaking the pan frequently until the bottom is lightly browned, about 7 minutes. Pour in the remaining ¼ cup of cream to allow the cream to flow under the hash. Lower the heat and cook 5 additional minutes or until the bottom is toasted and crisp. Sprinkle with parsley before serving.

SERVES 4 to 6

Jerked Chicken Breast

I bunch green onions (greens only), thinly sliced (about ½ cup)

2 medium onions, chopped (about 2½ cups)

4 large cloves garlic, minced

2 tablespoons finely minced gingerroot

I to 2 Scotch bonnet or habañero chiles, seeded and finely minced (2 to 3 tablespoons)

2 tablespoons dark brown sugar

I tablespoon ground allspice

I teaspoon ground black pepper

I teaspoon hot pepper sauce

I teaspoon ground cinnamon

I teaspoon dried thyme leaves, crushed

I teaspoon salt

½ teaspoon grated nutmeg

½ cup orange juice

½ cup seasoned rice vinegar

¼ cup red wine vinegar

¼ cup soy sauce

⅓ cup olive oil or vegetable oil

5 to 6 boneless, skinless chicken breast halves

1. Combine the green onion, chopped onion, garlic, gingerroot, and chile in a bowl. Set aside.

2. In a second bowl, mix together the brown sugar, allspice, black pepper, hot sauce, cinnamon, thyme, salt, and nutmeg. Whisk in the orange juice, vinegars, and soy sauce. Slowly drizzle in the oil while constantly whisking. Pour into the reserved green onion-ginger mixture, stirring to combine. Let the marinade stand for at least 1 hour. Cover and refrigerate until ready to use.

3. Place the chicken breasts into a ½-gallon plastic storage bag; pour in the marinade, mixing to coat well. Seal the bag and refrigerate overnight. Grill the chicken breasts over hot coals for approximately 8 minutes on each side. Remove from the grill and serve.

AFRICAN
AMERICAN

SERVES 6

Chicken 'n Dumplings

1 small stewing fowl (about 3½ pounds), rinsed

1 teaspoon celery salt

1 teaspoon onion salt

1 teaspoon dried basil, crushed

½ teaspoon dried marjoram

3 bay leaves

2 cups half-and-half

¼ cup cornstarch

Salt and ground black pepper

DUMPLINGS

1 cup all-purpose flour

¼ teaspoon salt

¼ teaspoon ground black pepper

⅓ cup chicken fat or other shortening

Chicken broth

1. Place the chicken in a pot with enough water to barely cover. Bring to a boil, lower the heat, and skim off the foam as it rises to the top. Add the celery salt, onion salt, basil, marjoram, and bay leaves. Cook, partially covered, for 2½ hours. While the chicken is cooking, from time to time skim melted fat from the surface of the broth until you have ⅓ cup to use for the dumpling recipe. Remove the chicken from the broth. Pull the meat from the bones and discard the skin and bones. Return the chicken pieces to the pot; cover to keep warm.

2. To prepare the dumplings, combine the flour, salt, and pepper in a small bowl. Add the reserved chicken fat and rub into the flour with your fingers until the mixture resembles coarse meal. Using a fork, blend 2 to 3 tablespoons of the reserved chicken broth into the flour mixture until it holds together and has the consistency of a soft, pliable dough. Knead 2 or 3 times on a board and pinch off 1½-inch pieces. Cover with a damp towel until ready to use.

3. Remove the lid from the chicken pot and mix in 1½ cups of the half-and-half. Bring to a gentle boil and drop the dumplings, one at a time, into the broth. Cover and cook 15 minutes, stirring occasionally to prevent the dumplings from sticking.

AFRICAN
AMERICAN

4. While the dumplings are cooking, mix the remaining ½ cup of the half-and-half with the cornstarch until dissolved. Pour into the chicken and dumplings, stirring to blend. Return to a boil, lower the heat, and simmer until thickened. Adjust the seasoning and thickness to taste, adding additional broth if necessary.

SERVES 4 TO 6

Peri-Peri Game Hens (Cornish Game Hens with Peri-Peri Barbecue Marinade)

2 dried red chile pepper pods (ancho, New Mexico, or guajillo), or substitute 1
  canned chile chipotle
2 fresh jalapeño chile peppers
½ cup hot water
6 cloves garlic, minced
½ cup cider vinegar
4 tablespoons lemon juice (about 2 lemons)
2 tablespoons Worcestershire sauce
1 teaspoon salt
1 teaspoon hot pepper sauce (optional)
2 Cornish game hens, halved

1. Using plastic gloves, slice the dried and fresh peppers in half and remove the seeds and stems. Place ½ cup of hot water, the chopped peppers, and the garlic in a blender container. Cover the blender and let steam and soak for 5 minutes to soften. Purée for 1 minute or until smooth. Open the lid and add the vinegar, lemon juice, Worcestershire, salt, and hot pepper sauce (if desired). Blend for 30 seconds and adjust the seasoning to taste.

2. Place the hens in a large, sealable plastic bag with the marinade. Refrigerate overnight or up to 24 hours, shaking the bag occasionally. Broil or grill 6 inches above hot coals, about 8 to 10 minutes on each side, or until done.

SERVES 2 TO 4

Spicy Fried Chicken

1 (3-pound) broiler-fryer, cut into 8 pieces
Milk to cover
1 ½ teaspoons garlic powder
2 teaspoons seasoning salt
1 tablespoon ground black pepper
2 teaspoons ground red pepper (cayenne)
1 cup all-purpose flour
2 cups vegetable oil

1. Put the chicken pieces in a large bowl and cover with milk. Refrigerate for 1 hour or longer.

2. Drain the chicken and shake off excess liquid. Mix the garlic powder, seasoning salt, and the black and red pepper; sprinkle the spices over the chicken so that the pieces are evenly coated.

3. Put the flour in a large plastic bag and add the chicken pieces, a few at a time, shaking gently. As the pieces are floured, transfer them to a wire rack or a sheet of waxed paper, placing them well apart from each other. Let stand for 20 to 25 minutes.

4. Meantime, heat the oil in a large, heavy skillet over high heat until it is nearly smoking. Add the chicken pieces in one layer; the fat should come halfway up the pieces. Cover and cook 10 to 12 minutes or until golden brown on one side; turn the pieces and reduce the heat to medium-low. Continue cooking, covered, until evenly browned on both sides, turning as needed. Total cooking time should be 20 to 25 minutes. As the pieces are cooked through, remove them to a rack to drain.

SERVES 4

Curried Lamb with Potatoes

1½ pounds boneless lamb shoulder

1 teaspoon salt

1 teaspoon ground black pepper

3 large cloves garlic, minced, or 2 tablespoons garlic powder

3 tablespoons curry powder

1 small jalapeño chile pepper, seeded and minced (about 1½ tablespoons)

1 medium onion, cut up (about 1 cup), plus 1 medium onion, cut into short strips (about 1½ cups)

3 green onions, chopped (about ½ cup)

3 tablespoons vegetable oil

2 cups hot water

2 medium potatoes, peeled and diced

1. Trim the lamb of any excess fat, cut into medium chunks, and place in a sealable plastic bag. In a mortar or blender, grind the salt, black pepper, garlic, curry powder, chile, cut-up onion, and ⅓ cup of the green onions to form a purée. Pour the purée over the lamb, making sure the chunks are completely coated. Refrigerate for 6 hours.

2. In a large frying pan, warm the oil over medium-high heat. Add the onion strips and sauté for 5 to 8 minutes or until they begin to brown. Remove the onions from the pan; cover and set aside. Place the meat in the hot oil and pan-fry, stirring occasionally, until completely browned. If necessary, add additional oil to the pan before searing the meat. Stir the hot water into the browned meat. Add the remaining green onions and any seasonings left in the sealable bag, and mix well. Bring to a boil, cover the pan tightly, and cook over medium-low heat for 45 minutes or until the lamb is very tender.

3. Stir the potatoes and reserved sautéed onion strips into the lamb. Cover and continue cooking about 20 minutes, stirring occasionally, until the potatoes are very soft and the gravy has thickened. Serve hot.

SERVES 4

Lamb-Stuffed Green Pawpaw

2 medium unripe pawpaws (green papaya), halved and seeded
1 teaspoon salt
2 tablespoons vegetable oil
½ pound minced or ground lamb
1 teaspoon seasoned salt
½ teaspoon ground red pepper (cayenne) or mild chili powder
1 medium onion, diced (about 1 cup)
2 large cloves garlic, minced
2 ripe tomatoes, diced, or ½ cup canned diced tomatoes and juice
½ teaspoon each allspice, ground coriander, and ginger
½ cup bread crumbs
Paprika

1. In a pot, bring 2 quarts of water to a boil. Add the papaya halves and ½ teaspoon of the salt. Cook 15 minutes or until just tender. Drain and pat dry with paper towels. Sprinkle the papaya halves with the remaining ½ teaspoon of salt and arrange them in a 13 x 9 x 2½-inch baking dish. Set aside.

2. Warm the oil in a skillet over medium-high heat. Add the lamb and sprinkle with the seasoned salt and cayenne. Sear, stirring frequently, until completely browned. Add the onion, garlic, tomatoes, and mixed spice to the lamb. Continue cooking, stirring occasionally, until the tomatoes have softened, about 10 minutes. Mix in ¼ cup of the bread crumbs. Adjust the seasoning to taste and remove from the heat. You should have about 2½ cups of stuffing.

3. Preheat the oven to 350°F. Fill each papaya half with about ½ cup of the meat mixture and top with some of the remaining ¼ cup of bread crumbs. Sprinkle with paprika. Bake uncovered for 35 to 45 minutes or until the papaya is tender when pierced with a fork. Serve hot.

SERVES 4

Osu Tsinalo (Broiled Beef Strips with Sautéed Mushrooms)

GHANA

2½ pounds boneless loin strip steaks, trimmed
½ cup Worcestershire sauce
1 tablespoon lemon juice
1 teaspoon Tabasco or hot pepper sauce
1 teaspoon salt
1 teaspoon ground black pepper
½ teaspoon dried rosemary leaves, crushed
1 teaspoon garlic powder
½ cup melted butter (about 1 stick)
1 teaspoon paprika
8 ounces mushrooms, cleaned and stems removed

1. Slice the beef into long paper-thin strips and place in a sealable plastic bag with the Worcestershire sauce, lemon juice, Tabasco, salt, pepper, rosemary, and garlic powder; thoroughly mix. Seal the bag and refrigerate at least 3 hours or overnight.

2. Preheat the broiler. Line the broiler pan with aluminum foil. Pour 2 tablespoons of the melted butter onto the foil and spread to coat evenly. Arrange the marinated beef strips on the foil side by side without overlapping. Brush the beef with an additional 2 tablespoons of the remaining butter and sprinkle with paprika.

3. Place the broiler pan 6 inches away from the heat source. Slowly broil for about 4 minutes until the meat is tender, turning once, allowing the steak to cook in its own juices.

4. Meanwhile, heat the remaining 4 tablespoons of butter in a small skillet over medium heat. Add the mushrooms and pan-fry, turning occasionally, until golden. Remove from heat. Serve the steak strips in their own juices with the sautéed mushrooms.

SERVES 4

Beef Pot Roast

2 tablespoons vegetable oil
1 (4-pound) boneless chuck roast
Salt
½ teaspoon pepper
1 bay leaf, crushed
1 large garlic clove, minced
8 small onions, peeled
8 small carrots, peeled
8 small potatoes, peeled
2 medium white turnips, peeled and quartered, or 1 small rutabaga (yellow turnip), peeled and cut into 1-inch cubes
¼ cup all-purpose flour

1. Heat the oil in a heavy kettle over moderate heat and brown the meat
well on all sides. Sprinkle with 1 teaspoon of salt and pepper; add 2½
cups of water, the bay leaf, and garlic. Cover and simmer over low heat
for 2 hours. Add water if needed and turn the meat occasionally.

2. Add the onions, carrots, potatoes, and turnips. Sprinkle lightly with
salt, cover, and simmer for 50 to 60 minutes, until tender.

3. Transfer the meat and vegetables to a bowl; cover with foil to keep
warm. Strain the liquid, adding water if necessary to make 1½ cups.
Return to the kettle.

4. Combine ½ cup of cold water and the flour in a jar with a tight-
fitting lid. Seal and shake vigorously until smooth. Slowly stir into the
pot roast liquid and continue to stir over moderate heat until the gravy
thickens and comes to a boil; reduce heat and simmer for 2 or 3 minutes.

5. Slice the meat (not too thin) and arrange on a heated platter with the
vegetables. Serve with the gravy.

SERVES 6 TO 8

Liver and Onions

1 pound beef or pork liver
2 to 3 tablespoons bacon drippings
1 large onion, sliced thin
½ cup all-purpose flour
1 teaspoon salt
¼ teaspoon pepper
1 teaspoon ground sage
¼ cup white wine or bouillon
1 tablespoon chopped fresh parsley

1. Slice the liver ¼ inch thick and cut into strips 1 inch wide and 4 inches long. Set aside.

2. Heat 2 tablespoons of bacon drippings in a large, heavy skillet and add the onion. Cook and stir over moderate heat until lightly browned. Remove with a slotted spoon to a bowl.

3. In a large plastic bag, combine the flour, salt, pepper, and sage. Add the liver strips and shake until coated. Fry the liver strips (in batches if necessary) for 5 to 8 minutes or until browned on both sides, adding more fat as needed.

4. When all the liver is browned, return the onion to the pan and stir meat and onions together. Add the wine and cook, stirring, for 2 minutes. Sprinkle with parsley before serving.

SERVES 4

Oven-Baked Spareribs

1 slab (about 4 pounds) lean spareribs, cut into 4-inch pieces
4 cups vinegar
2 large cloves garlic, minced
1 cup firmly packed brown sugar
2 teaspoons coarsely ground black pepper
½ teaspoon dried red pepper flakes
1 teaspoon salt

1. Rinse the ribs in cold water and drain. Place in a large bowl and add the vinegar, garlic, brown sugar, black pepper, red pepper flakes, and salt. Stir to mix thoroughly. Cover with plastic wrap and refrigerate overnight.

2. Preheat the oven to 450°F.

3. Drain the ribs, reserving the marinade, and arrange them in one layer in one or two baking pans. Pour 1 cup of the marinade over the ribs and bake for 30 minutes or until browned on both sides. Reduce the heat to 350°F and continue to cook, basting occasionally, for 1½ hours longer, until very tender.

SERVES 4

Barbecued Spareribs

2 slabs (about 3 to 4 pounds per person) pork loin ribs or spareribs
2 cups cider vinegar
½ cup soy sauce
1 tablespoon Mixed Spice (see page 164)
1 teaspoon ground red pepper (cayenne)
Juice of 2 lemons

1. Rinse the slabs under cold running water and wipe them clean; pat dry. Place the slabs in a pan large enough to marinate them in one layer.

2. Combine the vinegar, soy sauce, mixed spice, and cayenne pepper in a bowl. Pour over the ribs, cover, and let marinate for 3 hours in the refrigerator, turning the slabs over every half hour.

3. Build a barbecue fire using charcoal briquettes and hickory wood. Meanwhile, soak 2 cups of hickory chips in water. When the flame subsides and the coals are smoldering, throw in a handful of the soaked hickory chips. Place the slabs on the grill. Cover and cook, basting frequently and turning occasionally, until tender, about 1 hour. Every 15 minutes add additional soaked hickory chips to the coals to keep the fire smoky. If desired, brush the ribs with your favorite BBQ sauce before removing from the grill. Discard any remaining marinade.

SERVES 4 TO 6

Barbecued Pork Roast

I trimmed pork roast (Boston butt, boneless arm picnic, or blade roast), about
  4 to 5 pounds
Olive oil
Brenda's Special Meat Seasoning Rub (see page 165)
Barbecue Dipping Sauce (see page 104)

1. Rinse the roast and pat dry. Rub the roast with olive oil, followed by a generous sprinkling of the meat seasoning. Place in a nonreactive dish, cover, and refrigerate overnight.

2. Prepare a charcoal fire on one side of the barbecue. When the coals are smoldering, place the roast on a rack directly over the coals and grill, turning occasionally, until browned on all sides. Move the roast to the opposite side of the barbecue, cover the barbecue, and smoke for about 3 hours, turning every 45 minutes and adding more coals as needed.

3. Remove the roast when thoroughly cooked and tender. Before serving, let stand 10 to 15 minutes, loosely covered with foil. Slice the roast across the grain and serve with the BBQ sauce.

SERVES 8

Pork Barbecue Burgers

BARBECUE DIPPING SAUCE
1 cup cider vinegar
1 cup ketchup
1 teaspoon dried red pepper flakes
1 teaspoon ground black pepper
⅓ cup water
Salt to season

BURGERS
Barbecued Pork Roast (see page 103)
6 hamburger buns
Mustard

1. Combine the vinegar, ketchup, pepper flakes, and black pepper in a saucepan. Stir in the water and bring to a simmer. Remove from the heat, season to taste with salt, and cover to keep warm. Makes about 2⅓ cups.

2. Slice 1½ pounds of the cooked pork into thin slices. In a small saucepan, combine 1½ cups of the barbecue sauce with the pork slices, stirring to coat with sauce. Cover and cook 5 minutes over medium heat.

3. Spread the bottoms of soft hamburger buns with mustard. Top each bun with hot pork slices smothered in the barbecue sauce. Dip the top bun in the sauce and place over the meat.

SERVING SUGGESTION: Accompany with coleslaw.

SERVES 6

Baked Sliced Tongue

1 (3-pound) fresh or smoked beef tongue
Salt
1 bay leaf
2 tablespoons bacon drippings
2 medium onions, chopped
2 large cloves garlic, chopped
1 stalk celery, diced
½ cup sliced green olives
1 cup raisins
3 cups tomato purée

1. Wash the tongue well in cool water and place in a large enamel or stainless-steel kettle. Cover with salted water, using 1 teaspoon salt to 1 quart of water. Add the bay leaf. Bring to a boil, skim off the froth, and reduce the heat. Cover and simmer slowly for 3 to 4 hours, until tender. Plunge into cold water for 5 minutes to loosen the skin. Slit the skin lengthwise from root to tip on the underside. Peel off skin; cut away the root, bones, and gristle.

2. Preheat the oven to 350°F. Slice the tongue ½ inch thick, beginning at the large end. Set aside while you make the sauce.

3. Heat the drippings in a large ovenproof casserole. Add the onions, garlic, and celery; sauté 5 to 8 minutes. Add the olives, raisins, and tomato purée. Simmer the sauce for 5 minutes.

4. Arrange the tongue slices over the sauce; cover and bake for 45 minutes or until the tongue is very tender. Serve with the sauce.

SERVES 6 TO 8

Coconut Shrimp and Jollof Rice

3 tablespoons palm oil (see Note)

1 medium onion, chopped (about 1 cup)

2 large cloves garlic, minced

¾ cup diced carrots

¾ cup chopped green bell pepper

3 tablespoons grated fresh gingerroot

1 to 2 jalapeño chile peppers, minced, or 1 teaspoon ground red pepper (cayenne)

½ teaspoon ground turmeric

½ teaspoon ground allspice

1 large fresh bay leaf or 2 dried leaves

1 (14½-ounce) can diced tomatoes and juice

2 tablespoons tomato paste

2½ to 3 cups coconut milk

1 extra-large vegetable- or fish-flavored bouillon cube dissolved in 2 cups water

Salt to taste

1½ cups uncooked medium-grain rice

1 pound medium shrimp, shelled and deveined, tails left on

1 cup frozen peas, thawed

Fresh cilantro and hard-cooked eggs for garnish

1. Heat the oil in a large skillet or heavy pot over medium heat until it begins to smoke. Lower the heat and add the onion and garlic. Cook, stirring occasionally, until the onion has softened. Add the carrots, bell pepper, ginger, chile peppers, turmeric, allspice, and bay leaf. Continue cooking and stirring for 5 minutes or until the bell pepper has begun to soften.

2. Stir the diced tomatoes, juice, and the tomato paste into the vegetable mixture. Cook uncovered over medium heat until the tomato juices have evaporated, about 2 minutes. Add the coconut milk and the bouillon cube dissolved in water. Stir to mix well; season with salt to taste. Bring to a boil and stir in the rice. Lower the heat to medium and cook uncovered for 5 minutes, stirring occasionally.

3. Mix in the shrimp; reduce the heat to low; cover and simmer over very low heat for 20 minutes without disturbing. Remove from the heat; add the peas and let steam covered for 5 to 10 minutes. Before serving, garnish with fresh cilantro sprigs and chopped hard-cooked eggs.

WEST
AFRICA

SERVING SUGGESTION: Accompany with Spiced Greens (see page 144) and Boiled Plantains (see page 134).

NOTE: If palm oil is not available, substitute vegetable oil, adding a little turmeric or achiote paste to color. The flavor will not be similar, but the oil will color the dish.

PALM OIL is the bright orange-red oil extracted from the fruit of the African palm. Its distinctive flavor and coloring are highly valued and used in West African stews, soups, gravies, sauces, and vegetable dishes. Palm oil is a highly saturated fat sold in jars at markets specializing in Caribbean, Asian, and African foods.

SERVES 6

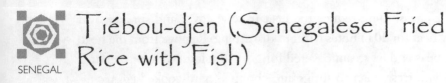

Tiébou-djen (Senegalese Fried Rice with Fish)

1 cup groundnut (peanut) oil
1 medium yellow onion, chopped (about 1¼ cups)
3 large cloves garlic, chopped, plus 2 tablespoons minced garlic
1 (12-ounce) can tomato paste
7 cups water
2 vegetable-, fish-, or chicken-flavored bouillon cubes, crumbled
½ cabbage, quartered and sliced (about 2½ cups)
3 carrots, cut into ¼-inch-thick matchstick strips (about 1 cup)
½ small oval eggplant, cut into short ½-inch-thick sticks (about 3 cups)
2 small cassavas, sliced into ½-inch rounds (about 2 cups)
½ cup loosely packed parsley leaves
2 tablespoons minced garlic
¼ teaspoon ground red pepper (cayenne) or ½ teaspoon ground black pepper
1½ tablespoons lemon juice
6 (1-inch-thick) bluefish fillets or red snapper steaks
Salt and pepper
1 pound uncooked jasmine or basmati rice (about 2 cups)
Lemon wedges for garnish

1. In a pot, warm the oil over medium-high heat. Add the onion and chopped garlic and fry for 3 minutes, stirring occasionally, until the onions have softened. Stir in the tomato paste and continue frying, stirring continuously, for about 2 minutes. Slowly pour in 1 cup of the water and one of the bouillon cubes, using a whisk to incorporate the ingredients. Lower the heat to medium and cook uncovered for about 20 minutes.

2. Add the remaining 6 cups of water, the cabbage, carrots, eggplant, and cassava to the tomato gravy. Bring to a rapid simmer and cook uncovered for an additional 20 minutes or until the vegetables are just tender.

3. While the vegetables are cooking, grind the parsley, the minced garlic, the remaining bouillon cube, cayenne pepper, and lemon juice together in a mortar or in a clean coffee grinder; set aside. Rinse the fish, pat dry, and generously season with salt and pepper. Cover and refrigerate.

4. With a strainer or slotted spoon, remove the cooked vegetables from the tomato gravy and place them on a serving platter. Spoon 1½ cups of the tomato gravy over the vegetables; cover to keep warm. Stir the parsley mixture into the remaining sauce in the pot. Add the fish steaks, and poach the fish over medium-low heat until the flesh is opaque, about 15 to 20 minutes, depending on the thickness of the fish. Remove the fish and arrange over the vegetables. Ladle 1 cup of tomato gravy over the fish and cover to keep warm.

5. Stir the rice into the remaining tomato gravy. Mix in just enough water to cover the rice by 1 inch. Add salt to season, if needed. Bring to a boil, lower the heat, and simmer covered for about 20 minutes. Remove from the heat and let stand covered for 10 minutes to finish cooking. Fluff the rice with a fork and mound on the platter with the fish and vegetables. Garnish with lemon and serve immediately.

CASSAVA, known also as yucca, is a tropical root vegetable with hard, white flesh covered by dark-brown barklike skin. In West African cooking, cassava is boiled and eaten as a vegetable; boiled and mashed into a porridge; or grated and dried, used as a staple food, similar to rice used in breads and dumplings.

SERVES 6

Chicken Thighs in Steak Sauce with Seasoned Rice

8 chicken thighs or 4 hindquarters (thighs and drumsticks)
Juice of 1 lemon
1 pound lean steak, cubed
2 teaspoons salt, divided
1 teaspoon ground white pepper, divided
1 teaspoon ground black pepper, divided
1 teaspoon ground sage, divided
2 teaspoons seasoned salt, divided
2 tablespoons ketchup, divided
4 medium onions, finely chopped (about 3 cups)
1 green bell pepper, seeded and finely chopped (about 1½ cups)
2 ripe tomatoes, chopped (about 1⅓ cups)
1½ teaspoons dried thyme leaves, crushed
⅓ cup vegetable oil
2 (6-ounce) cans tomato paste
2 cups uncooked long-grain rice
1 cabbage, quartered and steamed

1. Rinse the chicken and pat it dry. In a bowl, combine the chicken pieces with lemon juice; toss and let stand for 5 minutes. In a separate bowl, combine the steak and ½ teaspoon each of the salt, white and black pepper, and sage. Stir in 1 teaspoon of the seasoned salt and 1 tablespoon of the ketchup; thoroughly mix until the meat is well coated. Cover and refrigerate until ready to cook.

2. In a separate bowl, combine the onions, bell pepper, and tomatoes with 1 teaspoon of the thyme, ½ teaspoon of the salt, and the remaining ½ teaspoon each of the white pepper, black pepper, and sage. Mix well and set aside.

3. In a large skillet, heat the oil over medium-high heat. Carefully—to avoid splashing—add the seasoned chicken and steak to the hot oil.

Fry, turning as needed, until the chicken is golden and the steak has browned. Remove to a platter and cover to keep warm.

4. Put two-thirds of the onion-bell pepper mixture in the same skillet used for frying the chicken. Sauté over medium heat for 10 minutes, stirring occasionally. Add one of the cans of tomato paste. Stir well to combine; cover and continue cooking for 5 minutes, occasionally stirring to prevent the paste from burning. Return the cooked chicken and steak to the skillet. Stir in 2 cups of water, mixing to make a smooth sauce. Add the remaining teaspoon of seasoned salt, cover the skillet, and cook for about 35 minutes. If desired, remove the chicken from the sauce and pull the meat off the bones. Return the chicken pieces to the sauce and discard the bones and skin. Cover to keep warm.

5. To prepare seasoned rice, combine 2¾ cups water with the remaining 1 teaspoon of salt, remaining third of the onion-pepper mixture, the remaining tablespoon of ketchup, and the remaining ½ teaspoon of thyme. Bring to a boil. Add the rice, stir, and bring to a second boil. Immediately lower the heat; cover and simmer undisturbed for 15 minutes. Uncover the pot (rice should have absorbed the water) and stir in ½ cup of the sauce from the chicken and steak mixture. Cover the rice and continue cooking for 10 minutes over very low heat. Remove from the heat and let steam undisturbed for an additional 15 minutes. Serve the chicken and steak sauce over the rice accompanied by cabbage.

SERVES 4 TO 6

Traditional Chicken and Shrimp with Spiced Jollof Rice

3 pounds boneless chicken breasts or boneless thighs
½ cup olive oil, divided
1 tablespoon garlic salt
½ cup finely chopped yellow onion
½ cup finely chopped green bell pepper
1 tablespoon grated fresh gingerroot
2 (6-ounce) cans tomato paste
6½ cups chicken stock, divided
½ tablespoon salt, divided
1 tablespoon ground red pepper (cayenne)
1 teaspoon dried thyme leaves, crushed
1 pound shelled raw shrimp (optional)
½ onion, sliced
½ teaspoon turmeric
2 cups uncooked long-grain rice
Minced parsley, chopped green onion, and minced garlic
Lemon wedges for garnish

1. Rinse the chicken, pat dry, and cut it into ½-inch cubes. In a 10-inch skillet, warm ¼ cup of the oil over medium-high heat. Sprinkle the chicken pieces with the garlic salt and fry in the hot oil until browned, about 15 minutes. Remove the chicken to a platter and cover to keep warm.

2. In the same skillet, combine the onion, bell pepper, and ginger. Sauté, stirring frequently, until the onion is soft. Stir in the tomato paste, 3 cups of the chicken stock, 1 teaspoon of the salt, ½ teaspoon of the cayenne, and the thyme. Mix well. Simmer over low heat for 10 minutes. Return the fried chicken to the skillet along with the shrimp and continue cooking uncovered for 10 minutes, stirring occasionally. Cover the pot and remove from the heat.

3. In a saucepan, bring the remaining 3½ cups of chicken stock to a boil and add the onion slices, the remaining ½ teaspoon salt, and the turmeric. Add the rice; return to a boil, cover, and reduce the heat to low. Simmer undisturbed for 20 minutes. Remove the cover and spoon half the tomato gravy (from the chicken) onto the rice. Stir to blend. Continue cooking the rice uncovered over low heat until the liquid is almost completely absorbed. The rice should have the consistency of a risotto.

GAMBIA

4. To serve, mound the rice on a shallow serving platter or bowl. Arrange the chicken and shrimp with the remaining sauce around the rice. Sprinkle the rice with a mixture of minced parsley, green onion, and garlic. Garnish with the lemon wedges.

SERVES 6

Spicy Nigerian Chicken with Spiced Jollof Rice

1 broiler/fryer chicken, about 2½ to 3 pounds, cut into 8 serving pieces
1 lemon, halved
1½ tablespoons garlic salt
3 red bell peppers, cored and cut up (about 3 cups)
2 jalapeño chile peppers, stemmed, seeded, and halved
1 large onion, cut up (about 1½ cups)
2 medium ripe tomatoes, cut up
1 cup groundnut (peanut) oil
2 bay leaves
½ teaspoon Nigerian chili powder or ground red pepper (cayenne)
1 teaspoon dried thyme leaves, crushed
1 (28-ounce) can tomato purée (about 3½ cups)
3 cups raw long-grain rice, rinsed and drained
1 extra-large chicken bouillon cube dissolved in 2 cups hot water
Sliced tomato and onion rings for garnish
1 (6-ounce) bag fresh baby spinach leaves, steamed
2 hard-cooked eggs, quartered

1. Rinse the chicken pieces under cold running water and pat dry. Rub the chicken with the cut sides of the lemon. Generously sprinkle with garlic salt; cover and refrigerate for 1 hour.

2. Combine the bell peppers, jalapeño peppers, onion, and tomatoes in a food processor bowl or blender container. Grind to a coarse texture, using a little water if necessary. Set aside. Makes about 4 cups.

3. In a large skillet, heat the peanut oil. Add the chicken pieces and fry over medium heat until golden, turning as needed, about 15 minutes. Remove the chicken to a platter and cover to keep warm.

4. To the same oil used for frying the chicken, add the blended pepper mixture, the bay leaves, chili powder, and thyme. Fry for 3 minutes,

stirring constantly with a wooden spoon. Pour in the tomato purée and mix thoroughly. Stir in the rice and bring the mixture to a boil. Slowly pour in the chicken broth, ⅓ cup at a time, stirring constantly with a wooden spoon, allowing the mixture to return to a boil before adding additional broth. Add the fried chicken pieces to the skillet. Reduce the heat to a slow simmer and cook uncovered until the rice is just soft, about 20 minutes. Arrange the tomato slices and onion rings over the rice. Cover tightly, remove from the heat, and let steam 10 minutes before serving.

5. To serve, spoon the rice into an oval dish. Garnish with the spinach and quartered hard-cooked eggs.

NIGERIAN CHILI powder is dark, brick-red in color, and extremely hot. An appropriate substitute is ground cayenne pepper, but use it sparingly.

SERVES 6 TO 8

Shrimp and Chicken Casserole

8 boneless, skinless chicken breast halves
1 tablespoon seasoned salt
4 tablespoons (½ stick) butter
1 cup chopped onion
1 cup chopped celery (about 4 stalks)
8 to 12 mushrooms, chopped (about 1 cup)
⅓ cup chopped parsley
6 slices dried bread, crumbled (about 3 cups)
2 cups mayonnaise
1½ teaspoons Worcestershire sauce
2 teaspoons prepared mustard
1 teaspoon curry powder
2 pounds medium shrimp, cooked and shelled
⅓ cup shredded Gouda cheese (optional)

1. In a pot, combine the chicken breasts with water to barely cover. Bring to a boil and add the seasoned salt. Cover and cook for 25 minutes over medium heat. Remove the chicken. Cut the chicken into bite-size pieces; cover and set aside. You should have about 3 cups of chicken.

2. Melt the butter over medium heat in a small skillet. Add the onion, celery, mushrooms, and parsley. Sauté for 5 minutes or until the onion is soft. Set aside.

3. In a large bowl, mix together the bread crumbs, mayonnaise, Worcestershire, mustard, and curry powder until thoroughly combined. If the mixture is dry, sprinkle a few tablespoons of water on it to moisten.

4. Spoon the sautéed vegetables into the bread crumb mixture, stirring to mix well. Fold the cooked chicken and cooked shrimp into the mixture and spoon into a greased 13 x 9 x 2½-inch baking dish. If desired, sprinkle cheese over the casserole. Bake uncovered in a preheated 350°F oven until thoroughly hot and golden, about 30 to 45 minutes.

SERVES 6 TO 8

Chicken with Spicy Couscous

1 broiler/fryer chicken, about 3 pounds, cut into serving pieces and rinsed
1 (14½-ounce) can diced tomatoes and juice
½ teaspoon salt
½ teaspoon ground black pepper
2 to 3 cups water
1 medium yellow onion, finely chopped
2 beef-flavored bouillon cubes
½ teaspoon ground red pepper (cayenne) or paprika
1½ teaspoons thyme leaves
1 (6-ounce) can tomato paste
2¼ cups uncooked couscous or 1¼ cups uncooked long-grain rice
2 cups frozen vegetables (carrots, peas, and green beans), thawed

1. In a pot, combine the chicken, tomatoes and juice, salt, and black pepper. Add water to barely cover, about 2 to 3 cups. Bring to a boil and skim off the foam. Cover the pot, reduce the heat, and simmer for about 30 minutes or until the chicken is cooked. Remove the chicken from the pot and let it cool. Pull the meat from the bones. Discard the skin and bones and return the chicken pieces to the liquid in the pot.

2. Add the onion, bouillon cubes, cayenne, thyme, and tomato paste to the pot; mix well. Bring to a boil; lower the heat and simmer covered for about 10 minutes.

3. Add the couscous and vegetables to the pot, stir well, cover, and heat until the couscous is tender and the sauce is hot. (If using rice, bring to a rapid simmer and lower the heat. Continue cooking over low heat for 20 minutes or until rice is tender. Remove from the heat and let stand for 10 minutes before serving.) Fluff the couscous with a fork before serving.

SERVES 8

RESPECT

So often when people encounter someone from a different culture, they tend to judge them from their own cultural perspective. Too often, differences noted are considered wrong or bad because they fall short of cultural expectations. A child can be made to feel "less than" by someone not of his culture—devalued and disrespected. Respect is a term that is often bandied about. It is sung about, preached about, and written about. It is not often handed out, however. To acknowledge another's existence is the beginning of respect. To acknowledge another's value and worth is at the crux of respect. To acknowledge another's difference and then to honor it is the goal of respect. To honor the values and traditions of another and have that honor reciprocated is the outcome of respect. More than knowledge, respect is acceptance. Think of respect as a bottomless bowl of savory rice. No matter how often we dip into it with our spoons or bowls, there will always be more than enough to share.

CHAPTER SEVEN

Rice, Legumes, Porridges, Dumplings, and Starchy Vegetables

Root vegetables, yams, taro, plantains, cassava, and sweet potatoes, along with popular grains, rice, black-eyed peas, and cornmeal, are transformed into porridges, dumplings, and steamed side dishes that provide a nourishing foundation upon which the elaborate sauces, soups, and gravies are poured. Creative vegetarian entrees in this chapter use hearty vegetables such as eggplant, okra, and pumpkin, and a tremendous variety of wild greens to create lovely sautéed dishes or rich stews.

Tuwo Ginkafa (Mashed Rice)

2 cups uncooked long-grain rice
4 cups warm water
1 teaspoon salt

1. Place the unrinsed rice in a saucepan. Pour in the warm water; stir and let stand for 30 minutes. Add the salt and stir the rice once again.

2. Bring the rice to a quick boil over high heat. Reduce the heat to low, cover the pot, and simmer for 20 minutes. Uncover the pot and remove from the heat. (At this point the water should not be completely absorbed. If the rice is dry, stir in ⅓ cup of boiling water.)

3. Using a potato masher or pestle, mash the rice to the consistency of a thick porridge. Cover to keep warm.

VARIATION: Before mashing the rice, add your favorite seasoning, such as garlic or onion powder, a dash of cumin, lemon zest, butter, or cream.

SERVES 6

Boiled White Rice

4 cups water
1 teaspoon salt
1 tablespoon butter or margarine
2 cups uncooked long-grain rice, rinsed

1. In a large saucepan, combine the water, salt, and butter. Bring to a boil; add the rice and stir twice to separate the grains.

2. Reduce the heat to low and cook covered for about 20 minutes or until all the liquid has been absorbed. Remove from the heat and let steam covered for an additional 5 minutes. Uncover the rice and fluff with a fork.

VARIATION: To prepare garlic-flavored rice, melt 2 tablespoons of butter over medium heat. Mash 1 large clove of garlic and cook in the butter until the clove is just turning golden. Pour in the water, season with salt, and proceed with the recipe as directed.

SERVES 6

Fried Rice with Okra

AFRICAN
AMERICAN

8 slices lean bacon, cut into small pieces
1 pound okra, stems removed, sliced into ½-inch rounds (about 2 cups)
½ cup diced red bell pepper
½ cup diced onion
4 cups Boiled White Rice (see page 121)
4 tablespoons tomato sauce
Maggi's seasoning (optional)
Salt and ground black pepper

1. In a large skillet, fry the bacon over medium-high heat until crisp. Using a slotted spoon or spatula, remove the bacon and drain on absorbent towels. Stir the okra, red bell pepper, and onion into the bacon fat and pan-fry for about 5 minutes or until the okra has softened.

2. Add the rice and bacon to the skillet and continue frying and stirring until the rice is evenly coated with fat. Stir in the tomato sauce and Maggi's seasoning, if desired. Season to taste with salt and black pepper. Serve hot.

MAGGI'S SEASONING is a liquid condiment used to flavor meats, sauces, dressings, marinades, and stews. It is similar in color to Worcestershire and is available at Caribbean or Hispanic markets or in the international section of supermarkets.

SERVES 4 TO 6

Jollof Rice

2 medium ripe tomatoes, quartered
1 medium onion, quartered
3 red bell peppers, cored, seeded, and cut into large pieces (about 3 cups)
½ cup vegetable oil
1½ teaspoons curry powder
1¼ teaspoons red chili powder
¾ teaspoon salt
1 teaspoon ground white pepper
1½ teaspoons dried thyme leaves, crushed
1 (6-ounce) can tomato paste (optional)
4 cups uncooked long-grain rice, rinsed
4 cups hot water
Tomato and onion slices

1. Place the tomatoes in a blender container followed by the onion and bell peppers and blend for 10 seconds, until ground into a coarse purée, adding up to ¼ cup of water if necessary.

2. In a heavy pot, warm the oil over medium-high heat. Add the blended pepper purée, curry powder, chili powder, salt, white pepper, and thyme. Cook for 8 minutes, stirring occasionally.

3. Stir the tomato paste into the purée until well blended. Cover the pot and bring to a boil. Add the rice and hot water. Return to a boil; lower the heat and simmer covered for about 20 to 25 minutes or until the rice has absorbed the liquid. Remove from the heat, uncover, and top with tomato and onion slices. Allow to steam covered for 5 to 10 minutes before serving.

SERVES 8

Spiced Fried Rice

AFRICAN
AMERICAN

8 thick slices bacon
1 cup finely chopped green bell pepper
1 cup finely chopped red bell pepper
1 cup finely chopped yellow onion
1 cup finely chopped celery
4 cups Boiled White Rice (see page 121)
½ cup finely minced parsley
Garlic salt or ground red pepper (cayenne)

1. In a large skillet, fry the bacon over medium-high heat until crisp. Remove and place on absorbent towels to drain excess fat. Crumble the bacon and set aside.

2. Drain all but 4 tablespoons of the bacon drippings from the skillet. Over medium-high heat, sauté the bell peppers, onion, and celery until soft, about 5 minutes. Add the cooked rice, fried bacon pieces, and parsley. Cook, stirring constantly, until the rice is coated with fat and thoroughly heated. Season to taste with garlic salt or cayenne pepper. Serve hot.

SERVES 8

Baked Sausage and Rice

1 pound pork sausage meat
1 (10¾-ounce) can cream of mushroom soup
1 (10¾-ounce) can cream of celery soup
1 (10¾-ounce) can cream of chicken soup
1 (10¾-ounce) can water
Pinch of ground sage
1 cup uncooked rice

1. Preheat the oven to 350°F.

2. Place a heavy skillet over medium heat. Add the sausage and cook, stirring to break up lumps, until the sausage is browned. Transfer with a slotted spoon to a medium casserole.

3. Pour off the fat remaining in the pan.

4. In the same skillet, combine the soups, water, and sage; mix well and stir in the rice. Pour the mixture over the sausage and place the casserole in the oven. Bake uncovered for 25 minutes. Stir. Continue to bake for 10 minutes longer, until the rice is tender.

SERVES 4

West African Red Beans

1 cup (8 ounces) pinto beans
1 ¼ cups chopped yellow onion, divided
1 teaspoon salt
¼ cup peanut oil
2 medium ripe tomatoes, diced
1 tablespoon tomato paste
1 large clove garlic, minced
¼ to ½ teaspoon ground red pepper (cayenne)
½ teaspoon ground black pepper

1. Running the beans through your hands, pick out any small stones or shriveled beans and discard them. Place the sorted beans in a colander and rinse under cold water. Soak the beans overnight in water to cover by at least 4 inches.

2. Drain the beans and place them in a 2-quart saucepan with 4 cups of fresh water and ¼ cup of the chopped onion. Bring to a boil. Cover and cook over medium-low heat for 1½ to 2 hours or until the beans are just tender but not mushy. Stir in the salt. Cover and remove from the heat.

3. While the beans are cooking, heat the oil in a heavy skillet over medium-high heat. Add the remaining 1 cup of chopped onion and sauté for 3 minutes or until soft. Stir in the tomatoes, tomato paste, garlic, cayenne pepper, and black pepper. Stirring frequently, cook the mixture until the tomato juices have evaporated, about 8 minutes.

4. Using a colander, strain the cooked beans, reserving the cooking broth. Stir the beans into the tomato mixture, adding up to 1 cup of the cooking broth from the beans. Season to taste and bring to a boil over medium heat. Cook uncovered until the sauce is the desired consistency.

MAKES 3½ CUPS

Red Beans and Rice

AFRICAN
AMERICAN

1 pound dried red kidney beans
2 to 3 tablespoons bacon drippings
1 large onion, chopped
½ cup chopped green bell pepper
¼ cup chopped celery
4 cloves garlic, chopped
1 (14-ounce) can tomatoes
5 cups cold water
¾ teaspoon dried red pepper flakes
1 bay leaf
1 teaspoon dried thyme
1 smoked ham hock or small meaty ham bone
5 cups Boiled White Rice (see page 121)

1. Pick over the beans, place in a large saucepan, cover with 2 quarts of water, and let soak overnight. Drain, rinse, and drain again.

2. Heat the fat in a large stockpot and add the onion, green pepper, celery, and garlic. Sauté for 6 to 8 minutes. Drain the tomatoes, reserving their juices. Chop the tomatoes and add to the stockpot along with the juice and the water. Add the beans, red pepper flakes, bay leaf, thyme, and ham hock.

3. Simmer, covered, for 1½ hours or until tender. Remove the bay leaf. Serve the beans on a bed of rice.

SERVES 8 TO 10

Ruby's Baked Beans

AFRICAN
AMERICAN

1 pound ground beef
½ teaspoon salt
¼ teaspoon ground black pepper
¼ cup chopped yellow onion
¼ cup chopped green bell pepper
1 (1-ounce) package chili mix
2 (8-ounce) cans tomato sauce
4 (16-ounce) cans pork and beans, drained
½ cup packed brown sugar
2 tablespoons Worcestershire sauce
2 tablespoons honey

1. Place the beef in a skillet and season with salt and pepper. Fry over medium-high heat, stirring frequently, until browned. Add the onion and bell pepper and continue cooking until the onion has softened. Stir in the chili mix and the tomato sauce and cook for 5 minutes, stirring occasionally. Remove from the heat.

2. Put the drained canned beans into an ovenproof casserole dish. Sprinkle the brown sugar over the beans, followed by the Worcestershire sauce. Spoon the meat mixture into the casserole and partially mix into the beans. Drizzle the honey over the top and bake uncovered in a preheated 350°F oven for 40 minutes.

SERVES 8 to 10

Red Beans and Ham Hocks

1 pound dried red kidney beans
2 smoked ham hocks (about 1 ½ pounds)
1 medium onion, chopped
2 cloves garlic, chopped
1 red pepper pod

1. Pick over the beans and soak overnight in 2 quarts of water. Drain, rinse, and drain again.

2. Put the beans in a large saucepan and add water to cover (about 2 quarts). Add the ham hocks, onion, garlic, and red pepper pod. Bring to a boil, cover, and reduce the heat. Simmer for 2 hours or until the hocks are fork-tender.

SERVES 4 TO 6

Black-Eyed Peas and Ham Hocks

1 cup (8 ounces) dried black-eyed peas
2 pounds smoked ham hocks, cut into 2-inch pieces, or Polish sausage
Chicken stock or water for cooking
2 stalks celery, chopped
1 yellow onion, chopped
1 green bell pepper, cored, seeded, and chopped
2 tablespoons tomato paste
½ teaspoon dried red pepper flakes
1 bunch turnip greens, rinsed and stems removed

1. Sort the black-eyed peas to remove any stones and rinse under cold water. Place the peas in a bowl with water to cover by 3 inches. Let soak 4 hours at room temperature. Drain and set aside.

2. Place the ham hocks in a kettle and add just enough stock or water to barely cover. Cover with a lid and bring to a boil. Lower the heat and simmer for 1½ to 2 hours, or until tender. Occasionally check the water level, adding enough hot water to keep the ham hocks covered with broth.

3. Add the soaked peas, celery, onion, bell pepper, tomato paste, and dried red pepper flakes to the pot. Cook covered over medium-low heat until the peas are tender and the sauce has the desired consistency, about 45 minutes. Adjust the seasoning to taste. Add the turnip greens and continue cooking uncovered until the greens are tender. Remove the ham hocks before serving and use for another purpose or serve separately.

SERVING SUGGESTION: Serve with a garden salad and some rolls for a complete meal.

HAM HOCKS are the lower portion of a hog's legs that have been cured or smoked. Used to flavor soups, bean dishes, and stews, ham hocks can be purchased in 2- to 4-inch portions in the fresh-meat or cured-meat section of a supermarket.

SERVES 4 TO 6

Moi-Moi (Steamed Black-Eyed Pea Puddings)

2 cups (1 pound) dried black-eyed peas
½ medium onion, cut up
½ cup vegetable oil
1 teaspoon salt
1 teaspoon ground white pepper
½ teaspoon red chili powder
3 medium-cooked eggs, coarsely chopped

1. Rinse and sort the black-eyed peas to remove grit or small stones. Soak the peas overnight in warm water to cover by 4 inches; drain. After soaking, if the beans are not soft when squeezed between your fingers, place them in simmering water for 15 minutes. Immediately remove them from the heat and drain. Do not boil or the peas will absorb too much water.

2. If desired, rub the peas between the hands under running water to remove the skins and "black eyes." Place the peas and onion in a blender container and purée into a thick coarse paste. Do not purée until smooth. Pour the puréed mixture into a bowl and stir in the oil, salt, white pepper, and chili powder. Mix in the chopped eggs.

3. Heat a tea kettle of water to boiling. Pour the hot water into six 1-cup custard cups or ceramic coffee cups and let stand 2 minutes to warm. Pour out the water and fill each cup with the black-eyed pea mixture. Cover with plastic wrap. Place the filled cups in a pot large

enough to hold 6 cups in a single layer. Pour in enough hot water to come halfway up the sides of the cups. Bring the water to a gentle boil; cover and cook 30 minutes. Remove from the heat and let the puddings steam covered for 15 minutes. To serve, loosen the edges of the puddings with a dull knife. Invert the puddings onto a serving platter. Serve warm or at room temperature.

NIGERIA

SERVING SUGGESTION: Serve with Spiced Greens (see page 144).

SERVES 6

Boiled Plantains

2 large green or yellow-green plantains
3 cups water
1 teaspoon butter or margarine
½ teaspoon salt

1. To peel the plantains, slice off the tips at both ends. Make a lengthwise slit through the peel. Pry off the skin by inserting your fingers
between the peel and plantain. Slice each plantain into 1-inch chunks
and place in cold water to prevent discoloration.

2. In a saucepan, bring 3 cups of water to a boil. Add the butter and
salt. Drain the plantains and put them into the boiling water. Reduce
the heat to medium-low; cover and simmer 10 minutes or until the plantains are tender when pierced with a fork.

3. Drain the plantains and serve hot with additional butter, if desired.

SERVING SUGGESTION: Serve boiled plantains as a side dish with West
African soups, gravies, and sauces or stews.

PLANTAINS can be purchased in varying degrees of ripeness at markets
specializing in tropical produce. For this recipe, select green plantains,
which are cooked and eaten as a vegetable. The yellow-green plantains
are an acceptable substitute, but do have a subtle, sweeter flavor.

SERVES 4 TO 6

Alloko (Fried Plantains)

5 ripe plantains (sweet, blackened plantains)
Salt to season
Palm oil or peanut oil for deep-frying
Alloko Sauce (see page 163)

1. To peel plantains, slice off the tips at both ends. Make a lengthwise slit through the peel. Pry off the skin by inserting fingers between the palm and plantain. Slice the plantains diagonally ½ inch thick; sprinkle with salt; cover and refrigerate until ready to fry.

2. In a deep fryer or heavy skillet, heat the oil to 380°F. Carefully drop in enough plantain slices to cover the bottom of the skillet. Fry until golden, turning once. Using a slotted spoon, lift the plantain slices out of skillet and place on absorbent towels to drain excess oil. Serve with Alloko Sauce.

VARIATION: To prepare this recipe Ghanaian style, sprinkle the peeled plantain slices with about 4 tablespoons of lemon juice; cover and re-frigerate. In a scalable plastic bag, combine 4 tablespoons of ground dried ginger, 1 tablespoon of ground red pepper (cayenne), and 1 table-spoon of salt. In small batches, drop the plantain slices into the bag and shake to coat. Transfer to the hot oil and fry until golden. Place on absorbent towels to remove excess oil and serve hot as a snack or to accompany African stews.

SERVES 8 TO 10 OR MAKES ABOUT 60 PIECES

Plantain Fufu

2 large green-yellow plantains
3 cups water
1 teaspoon butter or margarine
½ teaspoon salt

1. To peel the plantains, slice off the tips at both ends. Make a lengthwise slit through the peel. Pry off the skin by inserting your fingers between the peel and the plantain. Cut the plantain into 1-inch-thick chunks and place in cold water to prevent discoloration.

2. In a saucepan, bring the water to a boil. Add the butter and salt. Drain the plantains and put them into the boiling water. Reduce the heat to medium-low, cover, and simmer for 10 minutes or until the plantains are tender when pierced with a fork.

3. Drain the plantains, reserving ½ cup of the cooking liquid, and place into the workbowl of a food processor or blender. Sprinkle with some of the cooking liquid and blend until smooth and the mixture pulls away from the side of the workbowl. Transfer the fufu to an ovenproof serving bowl; cover and keep warm in a 200°F oven until ready to serve.

SERVING SUGGESTION: Serve with stews, soups, and sauces.

MAKES ABOUT EIGHTEEN 1½-INCH BALLS

Yam and Sweet Potato Fufu

1 pound yams, peeled (see below)
1 teaspoon salt
1 pound sweet potatoes, peeled (2 to 3 medium)

1. Place whole peeled yams in a pot with salt and enough water to cover by 2 inches. Bring to a boil and cook uncovered over medium-high heat until the yams begin to soften. The cooking time will vary depending on size.

2. Add the peeled sweet potatoes to the same pot and continue cooking for about 15 minutes. Remove each yam and sweet potato when tender. Check for doneness by piercing with a knife. Do not let overcook or yams and sweet potatoes will absorb too much water.

3. To prepare fufu in the traditional method, place the drained yams and sweet potatoes in a wooden bowl. Pound the yams and sweet potatoes with a mallet in small batches until smooth and satiny. Continue mixing and mashing until doughlike. Do not add water. (Or you may use a food processor and process until the mixture pulls away from the sides of the workbowl.) Mound the fufu into desired sizes and shapes.

SERVING SUGGESTION: Serve with stews, soups, or vegetable sauces.

YAM (ÑAME) is a term often used in the United States for the moist, dark orange variety of sweet potato. True yams are seldom grown in the U.S. but can be found in most Hispanic markets; they are usually cut into chunks and sold by weight.

MAKES TWO 5-INCH MOUNDS OR TWENTY 1-INCH BALLS

Quick Fufu Dumplings (Foo Foo)

2 cups water, plus additional hot water as needed
½ teaspoon salt
1½ cups Cream of Wheat
1 cup potato flakes
⅓ cup minced parsley (optional)
1 tablespoon butter or margarine

1. In a saucepan, bring the water and salt to a boil over high heat. Reduce the heat to medium-low and whisk in the Cream of Wheat, ½ cup at a time. If the mixture gets too thick before incorporating the remaining Cream of Wheat, stir in a few tablespoons of additional hot water.

2. Continue to cook and stir constantly while adding the potato flakes, ½ cup at a time, along with 1 tablespoon of hot water. Add the parsley (if desired) and the butter and stir until the butter has melted. Continue cooking, stirring vigorously, until the fufu pulls away from the sides of the pan and forms a large ball.

3. When cool enough to handle, divide the fufu into 20 equal portions. Roll them into balls and serve as dumplings in a warm dish with your favorite sauce, soup, or stew.

MAKES TWENTY 1-INCH DUMPLINGS

Pap (Akamu, Fermented Corn Porridge)

2 cups cornmeal
2 cups water
1 cup milk
Sugar

1. In a glass bowl, combine the cornmeal with water. Loosely cover and place in a cool room to ferment, about 3 to 4 days. The cornmeal has fermented when you notice a sour smell. (The cornmeal will have settled to the bottom of the bowl.)

2. To prepare the pap, spoon out 2 heaping tablespoons of fermented cornmeal and 1 tablespoon of its water into a custard cup. Mix into a paste and set aside.

3. In a small saucepan, bring the milk to a rapid simmer over medium heat. Stir in the fermented cornmeal–water mixture and cook to the consistency of Cream of Wheat. Add sugar to taste.

SERVING SUGGESTION: Serve with Akara (Shrimp and Black-Eyed Pea Fritters, page 30) for a traditional Nigerian breakfast.

MAKES 3 CUPS

Extra-Rich Hominy Grits

4 cups water
½ teaspoon salt
1½ cups stone-ground hominy grits (coarsely ground dried white hominy)
½ cup milk or half-and-half
4 tablespoons (½ stick) butter or margarine (optional)
¾ cup shredded Cheddar cheese

1. In a saucepan, bring the water and salt to a boil. Quickly whisk in the grits to prevent lumps from forming and cook for 2 minutes, stirring constantly. Reduce the heat to medium-low and cook, stirring frequently, until thick, about 10 minutes for quick-to-cook grits and 30 minutes for regular grits. (At this point, the consistency should be thick enough to hold up a wooden spoon.)

2. Add the milk and butter to the grits and stir until smooth and creamy. Add the cheese and stir until completely melted.

SERVING SUGGESTION: Serve hot as a side dish or pour into a greased loaf pan and chill. The chilled hominy grits loaf can be sliced, then baked or fried.

VARIATION: Omit the butter and cheese for a more traditional version of hominy grits.

HOMINY GRITS are dried white hominy kernels that have been finely to coarsely ground or broken. Grits are generally simmered with water or milk until very thick and served as a side dish for breakfast or dinner. The cooked grits can also be poured into a greased loaf pan and chilled. The grits loaf can be sliced, then baked or fried.

SERVES 8

Banku (Cornmeal Dumplings)

GHANA

Traditionally, banku is made with fermented corn (maize) and/or cassava dough. These traditional dumplings are generally made without spices or herbs and served in spicy sauces or savory stews. This modern variation uses cornmeal and spices.

2 cups water
1 teaspoon salt
1 cup yellow cornmeal
½ cup semolina flour
1 teaspoon sugar
2 tablespoons chopped chives or 1 tablespoon Mixed Spice (see page 164)
2 tablespoons butter

1. Bring the water and salt to a boil in a medium saucepan. Quickly whisk in the cornmeal, followed by the flour, sugar, and chives. Reduce the heat and cook 5 minutes, stirring constantly and pressing the mixture against the sides of the pan with a wooden spoon. When the mixture follows the spoon around the pan, remove from the heat.

2. Place the cooked dough on a board and, when cool enough to handle, knead a few times until smooth. Divide into 18 equal-sized pieces and form into balls. Cover with a damp cloth to keep moist.

SERVING SUGGESTION: Serve with sauce, soups, or stews.

VARIATION: These dumplings can also be fried until golden and served in a spicy sauce of your choice. For a savory treat, stir 1 cup of shredded cheese into the hot cooked dough until it is melted and thoroughly combined. Knead and form into balls. Deep-fry in hot oil for 4 to 5 minutes or until golden. Remove with a slotted spoon, drain on paper towels, and serve hot.

MAKES ABOUT TWENTY 1-INCH DUMPLINGS

FAITH

"Faith, the substance of things hoped for, the evidence of things not seen." A roux is simple to make: flour, water, butter, heat. A people's faith is just as simple . . . an individual, belief, values, gratitude. If you feel your life lacks substance and weight, stir in a little faith. It will add a rich and lasting flavor to your life.

CHAPTER EIGHT

Vegetables and Accents

The basic condiments, sauces, and marinades that serve to accent West African dishes are usually pungent, hot and spicy, or aromatic—or a combination of all three. Commonly used vegetables include leafy greens, eggplant, bell peppers, okra, and green beans, which are most often served in a one-pot stew rather than as a separate course.

Jamma Jamma (Spiced Greens)

2 large bunches (about 2 pounds) mustard greens, collards, or chard
3 tablespoons vegetable oil
3 large cloves garlic, minced
½ onion, slivered
¼ to ½ teaspoon Nigerian dark chili powder or ground red pepper (cayenne)
¼ cup broth or water
Salt

1. Remove the stalks from the mustard greens and discard. Rinse the leaves thoroughly, shaking to remove excess water. Tear the leaves into large pieces, which should measure out to about 4 cups loosely packed.

2. In a large nonstick skillet, warm the oil over medium-high heat. Add the garlic and onion and sauté until soft, about 3 minutes. Add the chili powder and cook for 30 seconds, stirring constantly.

3. Finally add the greens and cook covered over medium heat, stirring and turning occasionally, until wilted, about 5 minutes. Remove the lid and add the broth and salt to taste. Cover and continue cooking until tender. Depending upon the variety of greens, this should take between 3 and 8 minutes. Remove from the heat and serve immediately.

SERVING SUGGESTION: Serve the spiced greens hot, as a savory side dish to grilled or stewed meats and fish, Jollof rice soups, and sauces.

NIGERIAN CHILI POWDER has a brick-red color and is extremely hot. Substitute ground red pepper if Nigerian ground chili powder is unavailable.

MAKES ABOUT 2 CUPS

Collard Greens and Neckbones

AFRICAN
AMERICAN

1 pound pork neckbones
2 bunches collard greens
1 tablespoon bacon drippings
Dash of Tabasco
Salt and pepper

1. Rinse the neckbones and place in a large saucepan with 2 quarts of water. Bring to a boil over high heat, skim off foam, and lower the heat. Simmer briskly, partially covered, for 1 to 1½ hours. Add water if necessary; you should have about 6 cups of broth. Remove the bones.

2. Trim off the tough stems and large midribs of the collard greens. Rinse well and drain in a colander. Chop or break into bite-size pieces.

3. Add the greens to the broth and cook covered over low heat for 1 hour or until tender.

4. Add the bacon drippings, Tabasco, and salt and pepper to taste. Serve with Corn Bread (page 50).

SERVES 4 TO 6

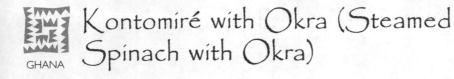

Kontomiré with Okra (Steamed Spinach with Okra)

2 (6-ounce) bags cleaned spinach leaves
1 teaspoon salt
¼ cup olive oil or palm oil
1 small white onion, chopped (about ¾ cup)
1 small green bell pepper (about 1 cup)
2 pounds small fresh okra, stems removed, sliced into ½-inch-thick rounds
¼ cup grated fresh gingerroot
1 large tomato, chopped (about ½ cup)
2 red jalapeño chile peppers, minced, or 1 teaspoon ground red pepper (cayenne)
1 extra-large vegetable or chicken bouillon cube dissolved in 1 cup warm water

1. Pinch off the large stems from the spinach greens and discard. Rinse the leaves under cold water until all loose dirt is removed.

2. In a pot, heat 3 quarts of water to boiling. Add salt and drop the leaves into the water. Return to a boil and cook uncovered for 2 minutes. Immediately drain. Chop the leaves and set aside.

3. In a skillet, warm the oil over medium heat. Sauté the onion, green pepper, and okra until the onion has softened. Stir in the ginger, tomato, chile peppers, and the bouillon cube dissolved in water. Bring to a boil; reduce the heat. Add the cooked spinach and stir to combine. Reduce the heat to low and simmer uncovered for 6 minutes.

SERVING SUGGESTION: Serve hot as a vegetable entree with rice, boiled yams, and Gari (cooked cassava powder, see page 73).

MAKES 5 CUPS

Okro (Fried Okra)

2 pounds fresh okra
2 eggs
3 tablespoons water
1½ cups yellow cornmeal
1 teaspoon salt
¼ teaspoon ground red pepper (cayenne)
3 to 4 tablespoons bacon drippings mixed with peanut oil for pan-frying

1. Slice the stems off the okra and cut the okra into ½-inch-thick rounds; set aside. In a medium bowl, beat the eggs with the water. Add the okra and toss until coated. Stir in the cornmeal, salt, and cayenne pepper. Mix well so that all the okra pieces are coated. Refrigerate for 10 minutes to set the breading before frying.

2. In a large skillet, warm the bacon drippings and oil over medium-high heat. Add half the okra to the hot oil and shake the pan so that the pieces separate. Do not stir the battered okra or the cornmeal coating will come loose. Fry until evenly golden, using a spatula to turn. This dish must be cooked slowly and carefully so that the okra dries out a bit in the cooking. Using a slotted spoon, lift the first batch of okra to absorbent towels to remove excess oil. Repeat the process and serve immediately.

OKRA, a vegetable associated with America's South, is actually indigenous to Africa, where it is used as the main ingredient in elaborate African main-course stews, rice dishes, vegetable dishes, salads, and soups. The oblong green okra pods have prominent ridges that run from the stem to its tapered tip. Cooking, especially in liquids, produces a viscous juice that flavors and thickens. Frying okra produces a bright green, slightly crisp, and flavorful vegetable.

SERVES 6

Eggplant Casserole

2 large eggplants
3 large garlic cloves, peeled
2 eggs, beaten
¾ cup heavy cream or evaporated skim milk
Dash of Tabasco
Salt and pepper to taste
1½ cups grated Cheddar cheese
1 cup fine dry bread crumbs

1. Peel the eggplants and cut into chunks. Drop the eggplant and garlic into a large saucepan of boiling salted water and cook until soft. Drain in a colander for at least 20 minutes.

2. Preheat the oven to 350°F. Butter a 13 x 9 x 2-inch baking dish.

3. Mash the eggplant and garlic. Beat in the eggs, cream, Tabasco, salt, and pepper.

4. Layer the eggplant mixture in the prepared baking dish. Sprinkle with half the cheese and then with half the crumbs. Repeat the layers.

5. Bake uncovered for 30 to 35 minutes, until set and lightly browned.

SERVES 10 TO 12

Honey-Glazed Carrots and Raisins

AFRICAN
AMERICAN

1 ½ pounds carrots, peeled and sliced thin (about 4 cups)
1 ½ tablespoons butter or margarine
1 tablespoon oil
2 tablespoons brown sugar
1 cup raisins
3 tablespoons honey
1 ½ teaspoons fresh lemon juice

1. In a saucepan, combine the carrots with enough water to cover. Bring to a rapid simmer and cook about 8 to 10 minutes or until just tender. Do not overcook. Remove from the heat and drain.

2. In a large skillet, melt the butter over medium heat. Pour in the oil and increase the heat to medium-high. When the oil is hot, add the carrots and sauté for 2 minutes. Sprinkle the brown sugar over the carrots, add the raisins, and cook, stirring constantly, until the sugar has melted.

3. Lower the heat to medium-low, cover, and finish cooking for 2 to 3 minutes, long enough to soften without overcooking. Meanwhile, combine the honey and lemon juice and stir into the skillet. Continue cooking uncovered, stirring for a few minutes, until the carrots are glazed. Serve immediately.

SERVES 6

Smothered Cabbage

1 medium head cabbage (about 2 pounds)
4 to 5 slices fatback
1 tablespoon sugar
1 tablespoon vinegar
Freshly ground black pepper

1. Trim away the outside leaves of the cabbage, then cut it into quarters. Break up the quarters with your hands.

2. Fry down the fatback in a cast-iron Dutch oven or other heavy skillet until crisp. Remove the meat and reserve.

3. Put the cabbage in the skillet, in batches if necessary, stirring over moderate heat until wilted, 8 to 10 minutes. Sprinkle with sugar and vinegar, cover tightly, and cook for 20 minutes, stirring occasionally.

4. Season with pepper and crumble the reserved fatback in before serving.

SERVES 4 TO 6

Corn Pudding

1 tablespoon butter
4 to 5 ears fresh corn, shucked
2 whole eggs
2 egg yolks
½ cup heavy cream or evaporated milk
2 tablespoons packed brown sugar
Salt to taste
½ teaspoon grated nutmeg

1. Preheat the oven to 375°F. Butter a 9-inch deep-dish pie plate or casserole.

2. Cut and scrape the corn off the cob. You should have about 2½ cups. Put the corn in a mixing bowl.

3. Add the eggs, egg yolks, cream, brown sugar, salt, and nutmeg. Beat until well mixed.

4. Pour the mixture into the prepared baking dish and bake uncovered for 25 minutes or until the pudding is set when tested with a knife. Serve hot.

SERVES 6

Oven-Glazed Turnips and Sweet Potatoes

2 pounds rutabaga (yellow turnip), peeled and cut into 2-inch chunks
1 pound sweet potatoes, peeled and cut into 2-inch chunks
½ cup firmly packed brown sugar
½ cup orange juice
3 tablespoons butter
½ teaspoon salt
½ teaspoon grated nutmeg

1. Put the rutabaga in a saucepan and the sweet potatoes in another saucepan. Cover both with cold water, bring to a boil, and cook until almost tender. (The rutabaga will take longer.) Drain.

2. Preheat the oven to 400°F. Butter a shallow baking dish and arrange the vegetables in the dish.

3. In a small saucepan, combine the brown sugar, orange juice, butter, salt, and nutmeg. Heat and stir until the butter is melted. Pour the mixture over the vegetables.

4. Bake uncovered, basting frequently with the pan juices, for 30 minutes or until the liquid is reduced and the vegetables are glazed.

SERVES 4 TO 6

Sweet Potato Puffs

2 pounds sweet potatoes, boiled and peeled (4 cups mashed)
¼ cup firmly packed brown sugar
Grated rind of 1 orange
4 tablespoons (½ stick) butter, melted
2 eggs, beaten
2 tablespoons dark rum (optional)
½ teaspoon cinnamon
¼ teaspoon grated nutmeg
½ teaspoon salt
4 marshmallows, halved
1 cup crushed cornflakes

1. Mash the sweet potatoes while still warm until light and fluffy. Beat in the brown sugar, orange rind, butter, eggs, rum, cinnamon, nutmeg, and salt.

2. Preheat the oven to 425°F.

3. Divide the potato mixture into 8 portions. Form each into a ball enclosing a marshmallow half. Roll the balls in the crushed cornflakes and arrange on a greased baking sheet.

4. Bake for 10 to 12 minutes. Serve immediately.

SERVES 8

Fried Green Tomatoes

5 large green tomatoes
Salt and ground black pepper to taste
1 cup seasoned cornmeal mix or 1 cup cornmeal with 1 teaspoon mixed spice
    and ½ teaspoon oregano
½ teaspoon ground red pepper (cayenne)
½ teaspoon garlic powder
3 to 4 tablespoons vegetable oil for frying

1. Rinse the tomatoes under warm water and remove the stems. Cut the tomatoes crosswise into thick slices (about 4 slices per large tomato). Generously sprinkle the tomato slices with salt and pepper. Set aside.

2. In a shallow bowl or platter, combine the cornmeal mix, cayenne pepper, and garlic powder until evenly blended. Dredge the tomato slices in the cornmeal mixture and place in a single layer on a cookie sheet covered with waxed paper. Cover and refrigerate for 10 minutes or up to 1 hour for the coating to set.

3. In a cast-iron or heavy skillet, warm the oil over medium-high heat. Just before frying, remove the tomatoes from the refrigerator. Pass each tomato slice through the remaining cornmeal mixture and place in the hot oil. Fry the slices 3 minutes per side, turning once, until golden brown. Serve hot.

MAKES ABOUT 20 TO 25 SLICES

Green Tomato Pie

10 to 12 medium green tomatoes, stems removed, sliced 1½ inches thick
½ cup sliced green onions (scallions)
¼ teaspoon dried oregano
½ teaspoon Italian seasoning
¼ teaspoon dried basil
¼ teaspoon ground black pepper
1 teaspoon salt
1 unbaked 9-inch pie crust
1 cup mayonnaise
1 cup grated white Italian blend cheese

1. In a medium bowl, combine the tomatoes, green onions, oregano, Italian seasoning, basil, black pepper, and salt. Gently toss to completely season the tomatoes.

2. Layer the seasoned green tomatoes in an unbaked pie crust. Spread the mayonnaise over the top layer and sprinkle with cheese.

3. Place in the middle rack of a preheated 350°F oven and bake uncovered for 35 minutes, until browned and thoroughly heated.

SERVES 4 to 6

Zucchini Pie

1 (8-ounce) package herb-seasoned stuffing mix
8 tablespoons (1 stick) butter, melted
2 pounds zucchini or yellow squash (about 6 cups sliced)
1 small onion, sliced
1 (10½-ounce) can condensed cream of chicken soup
1 cup sour cream
1 cup grated carrots (2 medium)

1. Preheat the oven to 350°F.

2. Combine the stuffing mix and butter. Press half the crumb mixture on the bottom of a 9-inch deep-dish pie plate or shallow casserole.

3. Slice the squash and onion and cook in boiling salted water for 5 minutes; drain in a colander.

4. In a mixing bowl, combine the soup and sour cream. Stir in the carrots; fold in the squash and onions.

5. Spoon the vegetable mixture into the baking dish and sprinkle with the remaining stuffing. Bake for 30 minutes, until heated through.

SERVES 8

Scalloped Summer Squash

AFRICAN
AMERICAN

2 pounds summer squash, sliced
4 tablespoons (½ stick) butter, melted
3 tablespoons grated onion
1 teaspoon sugar
Salt and pepper to taste

T O P P I N G
½ cup cracker crumbs mixed with 2 tablespoons melted butter

1. Preheat the oven to 350°F. Butter a 9-inch deep-dish pie plate or shallow casserole.

2. Cook the squash in a large saucepan of boiling salted water for 7 to 10 minutes, until tender. Drain thoroughly; mash with a potato masher.

3. Add the butter, onion, sugar, salt, and pepper; mix well. Pour into the prepared baking dish and sprinkle with the topping.

4. Bake uncovered for 25 to 30 minutes or until lightly browned.

SERVES 4

Creamed Squash

3 to 4 yellow squash, sliced
¼ cup chopped green onions (scallions), white portion only
1 tablespoon butter or margarine
½ teaspoon salt
¼ teaspoon ground black pepper
¼ cup cornstarch
½ cup milk
¼ cup shredded white cheese

1. Combine the squash, onion, butter, salt, and pepper in a 2-quart saucepan with water to barely cover. Bring to a boil; reduce the heat to medium and cook until the squash is tender, about 15 minutes.

2. Dissolve the cornstarch in the milk. Slowly pour the mixture one third at a time into the cooked squash, stirring until completely blended. Continue cooking, stirring frequently, until the sauce has thickened. If desired, mash the squash to the desired consistency and adjust the seasoning to taste. Sprinkle with cheese before serving.

SERVES 2

Chile Sambal (Dark Chile Shrimp Condiment)

1 cup vegetable oil
6 cloves garlic, minced
2 cups chopped yellow onion
¼ cup grated fresh gingerroot
¼ to ½ cup small dried prawns, ground into powder
½ cup ketchup or tomato purée
1 extra-large beef bouillon cube dissolved in 1 cup hot water
2 tablespoons ground red pepper (cayenne) or mild chili powder

1. Heat the oil in a cast-iron skillet over medium heat. Fry the garlic, onion, and ginger until the onion is soft. Stir in the ground prawns and cook until thickened, about 2 minutes.

2. In a small bowl, mix together the ketchup, dissolved bouillon cube, and cayenne. Add to the prawn mixture and cook for 5 minutes, stirring frequently. Season to taste with additional chili powder, if desired. Remove from the heat and pour into a serving bowl or storage jar or sealable plastic bags.

SERVING SUGGESTION: Use Chile Sambal as a condiment with fish, beef, chicken, and hamburgers, and as a seasoning for stews and sauces.

MAKES 3 CUPS

Hummus (Chick-Pea Spread)

2 large cloves garlic, crushed
Juice of 1 lemon
½ teaspoon salt
½ teaspoon ground red pepper (cayenne)
2 cups cooked or canned chick-peas (garbanzos), drained and rinsed
3 tablespoons sesame seed paste
⅓ cup vegetable oil

1. Place the garlic, lemon juice, salt, and cayenne in a mortar and grind into a paste. Combine the chick-peas and the sesame paste in a blender container and purée until smooth. While running the blender, slowly drizzle in the oil until the hummus is creamy yet spreadable. Adjust seasoning to taste.

2. Serve with triangles of flat bread or use as a condiment with boiled cassava, sweet potatoes, or plantains.

MAKES ABOUT 1¾ CUPS

Red Pepper Dipping Sauce

1 to 2 red jalapeño chile peppers, stems and seeds removed
½ teaspoon salt
2 large cloves garlic
1 red bell pepper, cored, seeded, and cut up
2 teaspoons white wine vinegar or lemon juice
1 tablespoon grated fresh gingerroot

1. In a mortar, grind the chile peppers, salt, and garlic to a pastelike consistency.

2. In a blender container, purée the bell pepper, vinegar, and ginger with the chili-garlic paste until smooth. Adjust seasoning to taste. Pour the pepper sauce into a small bowl and serve at room temperature.

SERVING SUGGESTION: Offer Red Pepper Dipping Sauce with Fried Plantains (see page 135).

VARIATION: For a simpler version of this recipe, combine the red bell pepper with 1 to 4 red chile peppers (based on your spice preference) in a blender container. Purée until smooth and add salt to taste.

MAKES ABOUT 1 CUP

Bajia (Red Chile–Coconut Sauce)

1 (12-ounce) bottle beer (see Note)
⅓ to ½ cup minced fresh chiles
3 medium ripe tomatoes, puréed in a blender (about 3 cups)
1 cup canned unsweetened coconut milk
½ teaspoon salt

1. Pour the beer into a bowl and let it stand at room temperature until flat.

2. Meanwhile, in a saucepan, combine the chiles, tomatoes, coconut milk, and salt. Bring to a boil; pour in the beer and cook for 5 minutes. Continue to cook, stirring occasionally, over medium-high heat until reduced by half, being careful not to inhale the chile fumes.

3. Remove the mixture from the heat and let cool to room temperature. Pour into a covered jar and refrigerate.

NOTE: In Kenya, this sauce is made with coconut alcohol.

SERVING SUGGESTION: Use as a condiment with rice dishes, fufus, stews, gravies, and roasted seafood and chicken.

MAKES ABOUT 2½ CUPS

Alloko Sauce (Spicy Fish Sauce)

½ cup vegetable oil

3 large onions, diced (about 5 cups)

1 large jalapeño chile pepper, minced

5 large cloves garlic, minced

5 cups diced ripe tomatoes (about 5 to 6 medium tomatoes)

1 (6-ounce) can tomato paste

1 tablespoon grated fresh gingerroot

2 bay leaves

1 teaspoon ground black pepper

2 tablespoons chili powder

1 ½ teaspoons salt

2 chicken-flavored bouillon cubes dissolved in 1 ½ cups water

3 pounds cooked whole fish, shredded (about 3 cups), or 6 ounces smoked
   haddock, shredded (about 1¾ cups)

1. In a large skillet or 2-quart pot, warm the oil over medium-high heat. Add the onions and sauté until golden. Stir in the minced pepper and garlic and continue sautéing until soft. Add the tomatoes and fry, stirring constantly, until the tomatoes soften and release their juices, about 10 minutes. Stir in the tomato paste and mix well. Season with the ginger, bay leaves, black pepper, chili powder, salt, and add the bouillon. Bring to a boil; reduce the heat to low and cook uncovered for 30 minutes, stirring occasionally.

2. Stir the fish into the sauce, adding additional water or fish broth if necessary. Cook for 15 minutes, or until the fish is hot and the flavors are well blended. Adjust the seasoning to your personal preference.

SERVING SUGGESTION: Serve over Fried Plantains (see page 135) or with Mashed Rice (see page 120), cassava, or boiled yams.

MAKES 9 CUPS

Mixed Spice Blends

MILD BLEND

1 teaspoon paprika or ¼ teaspoon ground red pepper (cayenne)

1 teaspoon ground cinnamon

1 teaspoon coarsely ground black pepper

1 teaspoon garlic salt

½ teaspoon crushed thyme leaves

SPICY BLEND

1 teaspoon Nigerian dark red chili powder or ground red pepper (cayenne)

1 teaspoon grated nutmeg

1 teaspoon garlic powder

½ teaspoon ground cinnamon

1 teaspoon crushed thyme leaves

1 teaspoon salt

In a small bowl, mix together all the ingredients in either the mild or spicy blend, adjusting a particular spice to your flavor preference. Keep in a covered jar.

MIXED SPICE is a common household ingredient that is made from a number of different seasonings.

Brenda's Special Meat Seasoning Rub

½ cup meat tenderizer
½ cup garlic powder
¼ cup salt
¼ cup ground black pepper
¼ cup monosodium glutamate (Accent) (optional)

Thoroughly mix together all ingredients in a bowl. Fill a large salt shaker with the seasoning and store the remainder in a jar with a tight-fitting lid. Use on all kinds of meat, such as Boston butts and pork chops.

MAKES 1¾ CUPS

TRADITION

Why does Uncle Pat make his famed sweet potato pie exactly the way Grandma Lottie did? And why did she make it the way her mother did? Tradition. Why does Cousin Mae give the family recipe for caramel cake to her co-worker but leave out that one special flavoring or spice? Tradition. Only family members are privy to the complete recipe, passed down from generation to generation, so that when you bite into that slice of pie, you are tasting exactly what your great-grandparents tasted, and there is comfort in that knowledge. Tradition helps us tell our story, and there is comfort in that knowledge too—a knowledge that explains where we came from, what we have done, and where it is possible to go from here. But more than knowledge, tradition is our value base. It provides a cultural base, as well, that keeps us connected to the past, the present, and future generations. Just as there are embellishments and adjustments to a recipe to make it one's own, so too are there in tradition. It is the duty of each generation to both pass traditions on and create new ones. Tradition gives a family its identity; tradition keeps a people connected.

CHAPTER NINE

Finishing Touches

Sweet fritters and fruit desserts reign
in this tropical kitchen. Papaya, banana,
mango, and ripe plantains are turned
into breads, cakes, muffins, fritters, ice
creams, sherbets, and frozen desserts
to alleviate the heat not only of the
climate but of the seasoning.

Old-Fashioned Caramel Cake

1 cup sour cream
¼ cup milk
⅔ cup (1 stick plus 2⅔ tablespoons) butter or margarine, softened
1¾ cups granulated sugar
2 eggs
1 teaspoon vanilla extract
1 teaspoon almond extract
2¾ cups all-purpose flour
2½ teaspoons baking powder
1 teaspoon salt (optional)

C A R A M E L   I C I N G
2 cups packed brown sugar
1 cup light cream
3 tablespoons butter
1 teaspoon vanilla extract

1. Whisk together the sour cream and milk in a small bowl; set aside. In a separate bowl with an electric mixer, beat the butter, sugar, eggs, and vanilla and almond extracts on high speed for 5 minutes, scraping the bowl occasionally. In a third bowl, whisk together the flour, baking powder, and salt. Reduce the beater speed to low and continue beating while adding the flour mixture (about ½ cup at a time) alternately with the sour cream mixture (about ⅓ cup at a time), beginning and ending with the flour. Do not overbeat; the batter should be light and fluffy.

2. Pour the batter into two 9-inch round floured pans. Bake in a pre-heated 350°F oven for 30 to 35 minutes or until a wooden toothpick inserted off center comes out clean. Remove the cakes from the oven and let cool in the pans for 10 minutes. Loosen the cakes from the sides of the pans with a dull knife and invert onto wire racks. Gently tap the center of each pan until the cakes are released. Let cool completely. Fill and frost the layers with caramel icing.

3. Make the icing while the cake cools; Combine the brown sugar and cream in a saucepan over moderate heat, stirring until the sugar is dissolved. Bring to a boil without stirring. Cover and cook about 3 minutes or until the steam has washed down any crystals that may have formed. Uncover and continue to cook, without stirring, for about 5 minutes, to 240°F. Remove from the heat and add the butter, stirring until melted; let cool to lukewarm. Add the vanilla and beat with a mixer until thick and creamy.

SERVES 6 TO 8

Fresh Pineapple Upside-Down Cake

10 tablespoons (1 stick plus 2 tablespoons) butter, melted
1 cup packed dark brown sugar
½ teaspoon grated nutmeg
1 ripe (very sweet) pineapple, peeled, cored, and cut into 1-inch rings, or
  1 (20-ounce) can pineapple rings packed in heavy syrup
1½ cups all-purpose flour
2 teaspoons baking powder
½ teaspoon salt
2 eggs, beaten
⅔ cup milk

1. Coat the bottom of a 9-inch cake pan or a heavy 10-inch skillet with 2 tablespoons of the melted butter; sprinkle with ½ cup of the sugar and the nutmeg. Arrange the pineapple rings side by side on the sugar. Set aside.

2. Preheat the oven to 350°F. In a mixing bowl, stir together the flour, the remaining ½ cup of brown sugar, the baking powder, and salt. Using an electric mixer, beat in the eggs, milk, and the remaining ½ cup of melted butter until thoroughly blended.

3. Pour the batter evenly over the pineapple. Bake for 50 minutes to 1 hour or until a toothpick inserted off center comes out clean. Remove from the oven and cool in the pan for 10 minutes. Loosen the edges of the cake from the pan and invert onto a serving platter. Leave the pan over the cake for a minute or two before removing.

SERVING SUGGESTION: Serve with fresh coconut ice cream.

MAKES ONE 9-INCH CAKE

Zucchini Tea Bread

3 eggs
2 cups granulated sugar
1 cup vegetable oil
½ teaspoon orange extract
½ teaspoon vanilla extract
2 cups grated zucchini
2½ cups self-rising flour (see Note)
1 cup uncooked oats
½ cup chopped pecans (optional)
1 tablespoon ground cinnamon
Powdered sugar for dusting (optional)

1. Beat together the eggs, sugar, oil, and the orange and vanilla extracts in a bowl until blended. Stir in the zucchini until evenly mixed. In a separate bowl, combine the flour, oats, pecans (if desired), and cinnamon. Stir into the zucchini mixture until the ingredients are completely blended.

2. Spray an 8-inch Bundt pan or a 9 x 5 x 3-inch loaf pan with vegetable oil cooking spray. Pour the batter into the pan, using a spatula to smooth the top. Bake in a preheated oven at 350°F for about 1 hour or until the loaf springs back when pressed lightly with a fingertip. Cool in the pan on a wire rack for 20 minutes, then turn out and cool completely.

3. Sprinkle the loaf lightly with powdered sugar before slicing, if desired.

NOTE: Instead of self-rising flour you may substitute 2½ cups of all-purpose flour, 1 teaspoon of baking powder, and ½ teaspoon of salt.

MAKES 1 LOAF

Peach Pie

AFRICAN
AMERICAN

PASTRY

3 cups all-purpose flour
1 teaspoon salt
1 cup solid vegetable shortening
8 tablespoons (1 stick) butter
1 egg beaten with ½ cup ice water

PEACH FILLING

8 to 10 medium ripe peaches
½ cup water
8 tablespoons (1 stick) butter
½ teaspoon ground cinnamon
1 teaspoon grated nutmeg
1 cup granulated sugar
2 tablespoons flour

1. Prepare the pastry: Stir the flour and salt together in a large bowl. Make a well in the center of the flour and drop in the shortening and butter. Using your fingers or a pastry blender, work the fat into the flour until completely incorporated and no longer visible. Slowly pour in the egg and water mixture while stirring with a fork; mix into the flour until a dough forms and sticks together. Place the dough on a floured board; knead a few times until smooth and divide in half, reserving 1 portion for the top crust. Roll one of the halves out to a ¼- to ⅝-inch thickness. Fit into a 9-inch pie pan; trim the overhanging dough to 1 inch larger than the pan; roll and flute the edges. Roll out the remaining portion of dough and slice into 1-inch-wide strips. Set aside.

2. Prepare the filling: Blanch and peel the peaches. Cut them in half and remove the pits. Cut each peach half into quarters or thirds, depending on the size of the peaches.

3. Place the peach slices in a small saucepan with the water. Bring to a rapid boil, lower the heat, and simmer uncovered for 5 minutes. Do not overcook. Add ¾ of the stick of butter, the cinnamon, nutmeg, and sugar, stirring until the butter has melted. Sprinkle flour over the peach mixture and stir to combine.

AFRICAN
AMERICAN

4. Pour the peaches into the unbaked crust. Overlap the pastry strips, creating a lattice top over the peach mixture. Dot the pie with the remaining ¼ stick of butter. Bake in a preheated 350°F oven until golden, about 40 minutes, being careful not to let the edges brown too fast.

SERVES 6

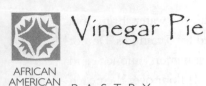

Vinegar Pie

AFRICAN
AMERICAN

PASTRY

1½ cups all-purpose flour
½ teaspoon salt
½ cup solid vegetable shortening
4 tablespoons (½ stick) butter
1 egg yolk beaten with ¼ cup ice water

FILLING

5 large eggs
1 cup sour cream
1 cup granulated sugar
3 tablespoons butter, melted
3 tablespoons cider vinegar
2 tablespoons flour
½ teaspoon ground cinnamon
½ teaspoon grated nutmeg
1 teaspoon vanilla extract
½ cup raisins

1. Prepare the pastry: Stir the flour and salt together in a large bowl. Makes a well in the center of the flour and drop in the shortening and butter. Using your fingers or a pastry blender, work the fat into the flour until completely incorporated. While stirring with a fork, slowly pour in enough water mixed with egg yolk so that a dough forms and sticks together. Place the dough on a floured board and roll out to a ¼- to ⅝-inch thickness. Fit into a 9-inch pie pan; trim the overhang to 1 inch and make a high fluted edge. Prick the pastry all over with a fork, cover with a sheet of waxed paper, and fill with pastry weights or raw rice. Bake in a preheated 425°F oven for 8 minutes; remove the waxed paper and weights and bake 4 minutes longer. Cool slightly while you make the filling.

2. In a medium bowl, lightly beat the eggs with a fork until just blended. Mix in the sour cream, sugar, butter, vinegar, flour, cinnamon, nutmeg, vanilla, and raisins.

AFRICAN
AMERICAN

3. Pour the filling into the pie crust and bake at 400°F for 10 minutes. Then reduce the heat to 350°F and bake an additional 15 minutes or until set.

SERVES 6

Chin-Chin (Sweet Pastry)

1 ¼ cups all-purpose flour, plus additional as needed
1 teaspoon grated nutmeg
½ cup granulated sugar
2 eggs, beaten
1 to 2 tablespoons milk
Vegetable oil for deep-frying
Powdered sugar for dusting (optional)

1. In a bowl, whisk together the flour, nutmeg, and granulated sugar. Make a well in the center of the flour and pour in the beaten eggs. Using a fork, mix the eggs and 1 tablespoon of the milk into the flour until the mixture has a stiff, doughlike consistency, adding the remaining milk if necessary.

2. Place the dough on a lightly floured cutting board and knead until smooth, adding additional flour as needed. Roll the dough out to a ½-inch thickness. Cut into twelve 6-inch-long strips.

3. In a deep fryer, heat sufficient oil to 380°F. Place several pieces of dough into the hot oil and fry until golden. Remove to absorbent towels to absorb the excess oil. Continue with remaining dough. Dust with powdered sugar, if desired.

MAKES 12

Banana Fritters

2 large ripe bananas, peeled and mashed
3½ tablespoons all-purpose flour
½ teaspoon baking powder
4 tablespoons granulated sugar
½ teaspoon ground cinnamon
1 egg, beaten
Vegetable oil for frying

1. In a medium bowl, combine the bananas, flour, baking powder, 2 tablespoons of the sugar, the cinnamon, and egg; mix thoroughly.

2. Pour sufficient oil into a large frying pan or deep-fat fryer and heat to 380°F. Working in batches if necessary, carefully drop heaping table-spoonfuls of dough into the hot oil. Fry 2 to 3 minutes per side, turning once, until golden brown. With a slotted spoon, remove the fritters from the oil and drain on absorbent towels. Immediately sprinkle with the remaining 2 tablespoons of sugar. Serve hot.

MAKES 12 FRITTERS

Holiday Sweet Potatoes

5 medium sweet potatoes
½ cup granulated sugar
½ cup packed brown sugar
2 tablespoons cornstarch
½ cup orange juice
8 tablespoons (1 stick) butter or margarine, melted
¼ teaspoon salt

1. In a saucepan, combine the sweet potatoes with water to cover by 2 inches. Bring to a boil, reduce the heat, and cook covered for 25 minutes over medium heat or until just tender. Drain and let stand until cool enough to handle. Peel the potatoes and slice into ½-inch-thick rounds.

2. In the same saucepan, mix the granulated and brown sugars with the cornstarch. Stir in the orange juice, melted butter, and salt. Simmer over medium heat, stirring constantly, until slightly thickened. Makes 1¼ cups of syrup.

3. Place the sweet potato slices in a greased 2-quart casserole. Pour the orange syrup over the potatoes and bake at 350°F for 35 minutes or until bubbling. Remove from the oven and let stand 10 minutes before serving.

SERVES 6

Sweet Potato Pone

4 cups grated sweet potatoes (about 3 medium)
½ cup packed light brown sugar
¾ cup milk
4 tablespoons (½ stick) butter, melted
¼ cup dark corn syrup
3 eggs, lightly beaten
1 teaspoon grated orange rind
½ teaspoon ground cinnamon
½ teaspoon ground ginger

Preheat the oven to 350°F. In a large bowl, combine the grated potatoes, brown sugar, milk, butter, corn syrup, eggs, orange rind, cinnamon, and ginger. Mix together until well blended. Pour the batter into
a greased rectangular 9 x 5 x 2½-inch loaf pan. Place on the middle
oven rack and bake for 2 hours and 25 minutes or until the top is
browned and the pone shrinks from the sides of the pan. Cool in the
pan for 20 minutes before turning out on a plate. Serve warm or cold,
cut into slices.

SERVES 6 TO 8

Baked Banana Dessert

LIBERIA

8 ripe yellow bananas

Peel the bananas and wrap loosely in foil. Bake at 350°F for 30 minutes. Open the foil and serve hot.

VARIATION: Pour 2 tablespoons sweetened condensed milk and 1 teaspoon fresh lime juice on each banana before sealing the wrap. Bake and serve as directed.

SERVES 8

Tropical Fruit Dessert

1 fresh coconut, grated or cut into thin slices (about 4 cups)
1 fresh pineapple, cored, peeled, and diced (about 8 slices or 4 cups diced)
1 fresh mango, peeled and diced (about 1 ½ cups)
4 oranges, peeled and thinly sliced
2 kiwis, peeled and thinly sliced
1 pint basket strawberries, stemmed and halved
3 bananas, peeled and cut into chunks
½ cup mayonnaise
Whipped or sour cream (optional)

Place a thick layer of freshly grated coconut on a large dessert platter, reserving 1 cup. Attractively arrange the pineapple, mango, oranges, kiwis, and strawberries over the coconut. Coat the banana chunks with mayonnaise and roll in the remaining coconut. Arrange on the platter. Serve with whipped cream, if desired.

SERVES 8

Marinated African Fruit Salad

NIGERIA

6 large ripe mangoes
4 medium ripe bananas, peeled and sliced
1 large ripe tomato, seeded and cubed
½ fresh pineapple, peeled, cored, and cut into chunks
Juice of 3 medium limes (about ⅓ cup)
¾ cup water
½ cup granulated sugar
¼ cup coconut liqueur (optional)
¾ cup shredded coconut
Mint leaves for garnish

1. Rinse and peel the mangoes; slice into random bite-size pieces. In a medium bowl, combine the mangoes, bananas, tomato, and pineapple; toss gently.

2. In a separate bowl, combine the line juice, water, sugar, and coconut liqueur, if desired, stirring to dissolve the sugar. Pour the sweetened lime water over the fruit. Cover the bowl and refrigerate at least 1 hour, stirring occasionally.

3. Before serving, gently toss the fruit and fruit juices. Spoon into fluted glasses, sprinkle with coconut, and garnish with mint leaves. Serve cold.

SERVES 6 TO 8

Ambrosia

1 (20-ounce) can pineapple chunks in light syrup
1 (17-ounce) can mixed fruit cocktail in light syrup
1 (11-ounce) can mandarin oranges
1 (10-ounce) jar maraschino cherries
3 cups banana chunks (about 3 small bananas)
2 cups diced pears (about 2 small pears)
Juice of 2 lemons (about ⅓ cup)
3 cups miniature marshmallows
1 cup sour cream
⅓ cup sweetened coconut flakes

1. Drain the pineapple, fruit cocktail, mandarin oranges, and cherries in a large sieve over a bowl. Transfer the syrup into a smaller bowl and refrigerate. Allow the fruit to drain in the sieve for 25 minutes, then place in a large clean bowl.

2. In a separate bowl, combine the bananas and pears with the lemon juice; toss gently and let stand 5 minutes, stirring occasionally. Add the bananas and pears with the lemon juice to the fruit mixture, along with the marshmallows and sour cream. Toss gently to combine. Cover and chill 1 hour.

3. Before serving, stir some of the reserved syrup to taste into the ambrosia. Garnish with the coconut flakes.

SERVES 6 TO 8

Thiakry (Chakrey)

2 cups water
Pinch of salt
1 (10-ounce) package uncooked couscous (about 2⅓ cups)
2 cups plain or vanilla yogurt
½ teaspoon vanilla extract
1 cup half-and-half
4 to 6 tablespoons granulated sugar
Mint leaves to garnish

1. In a saucepan, heat the water with the salt to boiling. Stir in the couscous and cover the pan. Immediately remove from the heat and let stand undisturbed for 10 minutes or until the water has been completely absorbed. Fluff with a fork and let cool.

2. In a medium bowl, beat together the yogurt, vanilla extract, and half-and-half.

3. With a fork, stir the couscous into the yogurt mixture until evenly blended. Add sugar to taste. Pour into tall glasses and garnish with mint leaves. Sip or serve with a dessert spoon.

MAKES 8 CUPS

Fried Custard

1 pint (2 cups) milk
2 cinnamon sticks
2 tablespoons flour
½ cup granulated sugar
1½ tablespoons cornstarch
⅛ teaspoon salt
4 egg yolks, slightly beaten
1½ teaspoons melted butter
1 teaspoon vanilla extract
4 egg whites
Saltine cracker crumbs
Oil for deep-frying

1. In a heavy saucepan, bring the milk to a gentle boil. Add the cinnamon sticks and cook for 3 minutes. Remove from the heat.

2. In a small bowl, mix together the flour, sugar, cornstarch, and salt. Remove the cinnamon sticks from the milk and whisk the milk into the sugar mixture. Continue whisking while adding the egg yolks, butter, and vanilla. Return to the stove and cook over medium heat, stirring constantly, until very thick. Pour the mixture into a 9 x 9-inch baking pan and chill in the refrigerator for 24 hours.

3. Shortly before serving, beat the egg whites to the soft peak stage. Cut the custard into cubes of the desired size. Dip each cube into the egg whites to coat completely and then in the cracker crumbs. Refrigerate for 10 minutes to set.

4. In a deep heavy frying pan, heat sufficient oil to 375°F so that the cubes will be completely submerged. Fry the custard cubes in small batches until golden and crisp. Serve hot.

SERVES 6

Baked Rice-Raisin Pudding

AFRICAN
AMERICAN

2 cups cooked long-grain rice

¾ cup seedless raisins

4 eggs, beaten

3 cups milk

⅓ cup plus 2 teaspoons granulated sugar

2 teaspoons vanilla extract

2 teaspoons grated lemon peel

¼ teaspoon salt

1 teaspoon ground cinnamon

2 cups whipped cream

1. Combine the rice, raisins, beaten eggs, milk, ⅓ cup of the sugar, the vanilla, lemon peel, and salt in a mixing bowl and stir until well blended. Pour into a greased 2½-quart baking dish.

2. Set a large pan filled with 1 inch of hot water on the bottom rack of the oven. Carefully place the rice pudding dish in the pan of hot water. Add additional hot water to reach halfway up the sides of the baking dish. Bake in a preheated 300°F oven for 1 hour. After 30 minutes, insert a spoon in the pudding and stir from the bottom up to mix the rice into the top layer of custard. Continue baking for 10 to 20 minutes or until a knife inserted off center comes out clean. Remove the pudding from the oven and place on a wire rack to cool.

3. In a small bowl, combine the remaining 2 teaspoons of sugar with the cinnamon. Spread the cooled pudding with the whipped cream and sprinkle with the cinnamon-sugar mixture. Brown quickly under the broiler, being careful not to burn.

SERVES 6 TO 8

Homemade Vanilla Ice Cream

1 ¼ cups granulated sugar
2 tablespoons flour
1 pint (2 cups) whipping cream
4 eggs
1 quart (4 cups) half-and-half
1 tablespoon vanilla extract

Mix together the sugar and flour in a heavy saucepan and whisk in the whipping cream. Beat the eggs in a small bowl until frothy. Gradually pour the eggs, half-and-half, and vanilla into the saucepan and cook the custard over medium-low heat, stirring constantly with a wooden spoon until thickened, about 15 minutes. Remove from the heat and set the saucepan in cold water until cooled. Pour into a freezer container; cover and freeze until firm.

SERVES 6 TO 8

Banana Ice Cream

WEST
AFRICA

2 (12-ounce) cans evaporated milk
1 cup water
½ cup granulated sugar
2 egg yolks, beaten until creamy
2 ripe bananas, peeled and crushed (about 1 cup)
Juice of 1 lime (about ¼ to ⅓ cup)
2 egg whites

1. Combine the milk, water, and sugar in a saucepan; heat to boiling. Reduce the heat to very low and whisk a little of the hot mixture into the beaten egg yolks. Slowly whisk the egg yolk mixture into the milk mixture. Continue cooking, stirring occasionally, until the mixture thickens to a custard consistency. Remove from the heat.

2. Purée the bananas and lime juice in a blender container. Whisk the banana purée into the custard mixture until smooth.

3. Beat the egg whites until stiff and fold into the custard mixture. Pour into a shallow bowl and freeze.

4. When the mixture is half frozen, place in a mixing bowl and beat hard until fluffy. Return to the shallow bowl and freeze until firm.

SERVES 6 TO 8

Pineapple Milk Sherbet

2 (12-ounce) cans evaporated milk
Juice of ½ orange (about 3 tablespoons)
Juice of 1 lime (about ¼ cup)
1 cup sugar
2 cups water
1 cup chopped fresh pineapple or drained canned pineapple tidbits

1. Pour the milk into a pitcher or bowl, cover, and chill in the refrigerator overnight. In a separate container, combine the orange and lime juices and chill overnight.

2. The next day, slowly pour the chilled fruit juices into the chilled milk, stirring until just mixed (the chilling helps prevent the milk from curdling). Add the sugar to the milk mixture, stirring to dissolve. Mix in the water and pineapple and pour into a shallow dish.

3. Freeze the pineapple-milk mixture until half frozen. Spoon the ice into a bowl and beat thoroughly. Return to the dish and freeze 4 hours or overnight.

SERVES 4

EMPATHY

A plaque made from the wood of the giant redwood is inscribed with a Native American prayer: "Great Spirit—grant that I may not criticize my neighbor until I have walked a mile in his moccasins." The ability to see the world through another's eyes. The capacity to feel with another's heart. The willingness to understand another's world view. Empathy. To try a dish that at first seems foreign, then to understand a people through the tasting—that is empathy. To be valuable. That is empathy. If you can do nothing else for another, try empathy. It will excite the taste buds of your spirit and satisfy your soul.

CHAPTER TEN

West African Food, Culture, and History at a Glance

GHANA

HISTORY

Ghana is the former Gold Coast, where more than 500 years ago European settlers came in search of gold and found it. Ghana was stripped of its natural resources and golden artifacts from the Ashanti people and other tribes. Forts were built along the coast, and the slave trade was big business among the Dutch, British, and Danes in the late sixteenth century. In the early 1920s cocoa became the backbone of the economy.

THE FOOD

Soups, which are really sauces, are the staples of the Ghanaian diet. These thick broths are eaten with a starch such as Fufu, Kenkey, or Banku. One of the most popular street foods is Kelewele, a spicy dessert of fried plantains in long chips seasoned with ground chile pepper and ginger. The Akoakyer festival is held the first Saturday in May, and the main event is the deer hunt. Groups of men try to be the first to catch a deer; this is followed by a royal procession and dancing in the streets. Ghana is known for its beautiful fabrics and is the home of the Kente cloth made by the Ashanti.

S E N E G A L

H I S T O R Y

Senegal is the most visited country in West Africa. Dakar, the capital of Senegal, is an interesting mix of Afro-French characteristics. Civilization can be traced back to 1300 B.C. in Senegal. European settlers made their mark on Dakar and settled in Île de Gorée, and the Portuguese captured slaves for gold and ivory. The brutality of that period lingers among the old slave caves and dungeons at Île de Gorée and other forts along the coast.

T H E   F O O D

Senegal is known for its fine cuisine. Favorite dishes include Poulet Yassa, grilled chicken marinated in a mild chili sauce, Mafée, and a peanut stew. Tiébou-djen (cheybou-jen) is the national dish and consists of rice baked in a thick sauce of fish and vegetables. Senegalese National Day is the biggest public celebration and coincides with the West African International Marathon held in Dakar.

THE FEDERAL REPUBLIC OF NIGERIA

HISTORY

Nigeria is home to one out of every five Africans. It leads Africa in all production, and six of the seven car-assembly plants are in Nigeria. During the late nineteenth century, Britain sent its armed forces to gain political control over Nigeria. Tin was big business, and the British wanted it. The British destroyed the independent tin producers, converting them into wage earners with no other means of support.

THE FOOD

Soup is common in Nigeria and is eaten mostly at lunch. Most Nigerians eat soup using their hands like a spoon. As in most African cities, only the right hand is used for eating. The left hand is reserved for cleansing. Favorite soups include Egusi Soup, a red-hot yellow stew made with meat, red peppers, ground dried prawns, and green leaves, and Palm-nut Soup. Palm-nut Soup is like a stew made with meat, peppers, tomatoes, onions, and palm nut.

If you can visit in late February, don't miss the Arqungu Fishing and Cultural Festival, a three-day festival that takes place on the banks of the Sokoto River. This international festival attracts persons from around the United States and the world.

CÔTE D'IVOIRE
(IVORY COAST)

HISTORY

Known as the "little Paris of West Africa," Côte d'Ivoire attracts Africans from all over West Africa, making it West Africa's most cosmopolitan city. Yamoussoukro, the new capital, was the home of the late Houphouët-Boigny, the first president, and is home also of the Basilique de Notre Dame de la Paix—the Basilica. The Fête de Masques, which is held in February, is one of the more famous celebrations in that region.

THE FOOD

A visit to Côte d'Ivoire is not complete if you have not experienced dining at a maquis (mah-key), an open-air market where braised chicken and fish is served smothered in onions and tomatoes. It is truly an Ivoirian food experience. Kejenou, an Ivoirian specialty, is one of the country's most celebrated special-occasion dishes.

Epilogue

THE WELCOME TABLE

by Dr. Dorothy Irene Height, President and CEO, National Council of Negro Women

Mother Africa's Table is heavily laden with the culinary creations of her people, a people who hail from Africa but who now call other places home. Her people are resourceful and creative in maintaining and expanding their cultural legacies. They are resourceful in their ability to bring parts of Africa to distant lands, creative in their ability to absorb new elements, thereby producing something entirely new, but still reminiscent of that distant land.

As the table groans under the weight of these old and new delicacies, a synergy is at work. Mother Africa's people—old and new, near and far—are more than the sum of their individual numbers. When they come together, something great and massive is achieved.

All are welcome at Mother Africa's Table. This is the gathering place where her people draw to laugh, to cry, to shout, and to celebrate. It is the flavorful repository of a people's historical journey.

The National Center for African American Women bids you welcome to Mother Africa's Table. Just like the family table, we will be the "nerve center" for idea exchange and action among African American women and their families who have clung to their faith and its rituals while in danger of being torn asunder. And finally, like this treasury of recipes, we will be the repository of information and resources for African American women's organizations. There is an African proverb that states, "There are three friends in this world: courage, sense, and insight." You will find all three at the National Center for African American Women and also gathered at Mother Africa's Table. Pull up a chair and join us at the Welcome Table.

THE NATIONAL CENTER FOR AFRICAN AMERICAN WOMEN

Mary McLeod Bethune's vision of giving African American women national voice and community responsiveness for social and economic justice is even more timely in meeting today's increasingly complex and challenging issues.

The National Council of Negro Women, under the leadership of Dorothy I. Height, has envisioned the establishment of the National Center for African American Women in Washington, D.C., to provide the primary resource and the crucial link to leadership, programs, ideas, resources, and education on all aspects affecting quality of life for African American women well into the next century.

Working under the NCNW umbrella, affiliated organizations will spearhead the drive to put into action the mission so relevant today: to recognize and meet the crucial needs of African American women and their families in the communities where we live and to represent African American women as an agent for positive change working with public and private sector leadership.

A vast clearinghouse of resources and know-how specific to addressing the issues African American women and their families face will be immediately accessible to communities via the Center's emerging databases and advanced communications capability.

The Center will provide an environment to bring the issues of greatest importance to the national forefront. Ongoing activities at the Center will underscore the valuable contributions African American women make to the fabric of American life. But most importantly, the Center will educate and keep leadership informed on the concepts, policies, and strategies for affecting positive change on behalf of African American women and their families. The Center will also provide a meaningful venue for the release of important findings, reports, and academic papers. Ongoing exhibits and seminars open to the public will make the Center an important cultural destination for visitors and residents of Washington, D.C.

The Center will also house the national headquarters of the National Council of Negro Women, which will work vigorously in the Bethune spirit and tradition to "leave no one behind."

Contributors

A. J. Akoto
Kay Lindsey
Stephen Leake
Ali
Regina Cordova
Christopher Gbemudu
Theodore Sahou
Dorothy Bodie
Inez Kitchens
Ngozi
Beverly J. Barnes
Aminata Koulibaly
Fatima Aliu
Louella Whitehurst
Tiguida Kaba
Theresa Okumabua
Joyce M. Blackmon
Emma Lincoln
Beneva Meaweather
Juanita Russell
Ruby Bright
Brenda Brunner
Gladys Jones
Emma Carter Brown
Sunbeam Hughes
Larry Price
Adelaide
Rachel Ode

Index